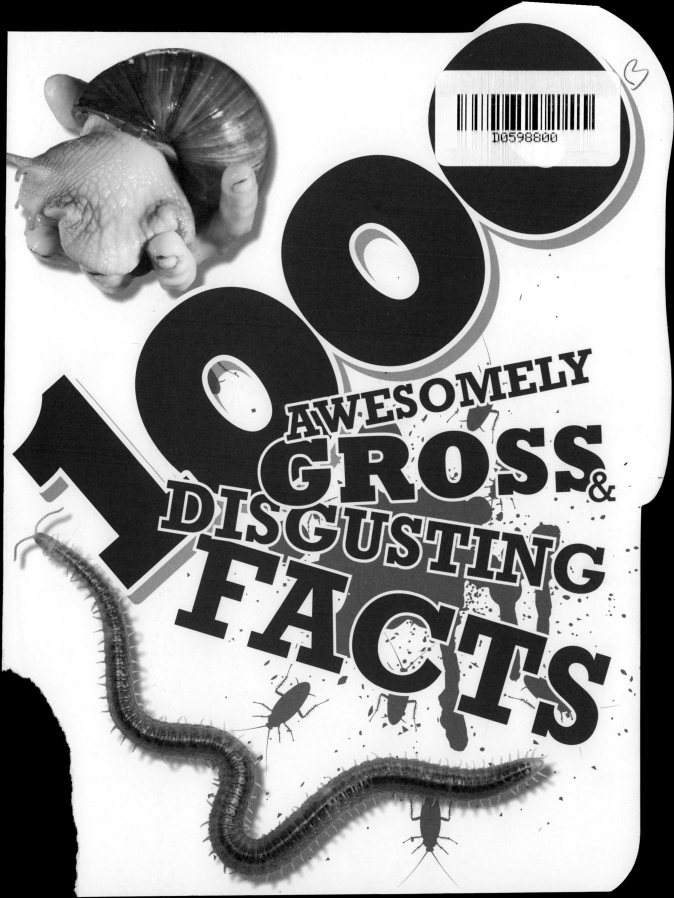

1000 AWESOMELY GROSS & DISGUSTING FACTS

D0598800

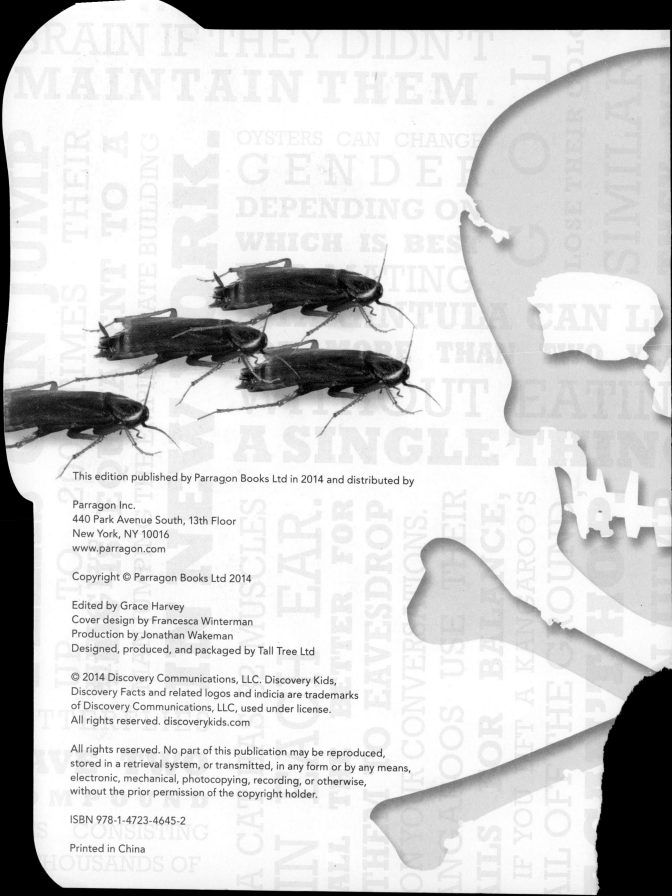

This edition published by Parragon Books Ltd in 2014 and distributed by

Parragon Inc.
440 Park Avenue South, 13th Floor
New York, NY 10016
www.parragon.com

Edited by Grace Harvey
Cover design by Francesca Winterman
Production by Jonathan Wakeman
Designed, produced, and packaged by Tall Tree Ltd

ISBN 978-1-4723-4645-2

Printed in China

Discovery KIDS™

1000

AWESOMELY GROSS & DISGUSTING FACTS

Parragon

Bath • New York • Cologne • Melbourne • Delhi
Hong Kong • Shenzhen • Singapore • Amsterdam

CONTENTS

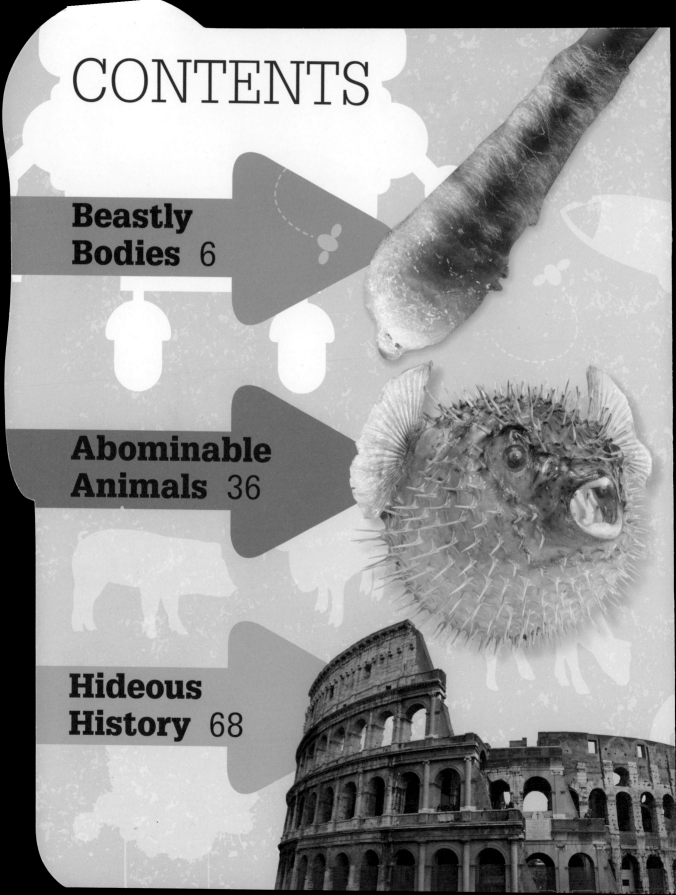

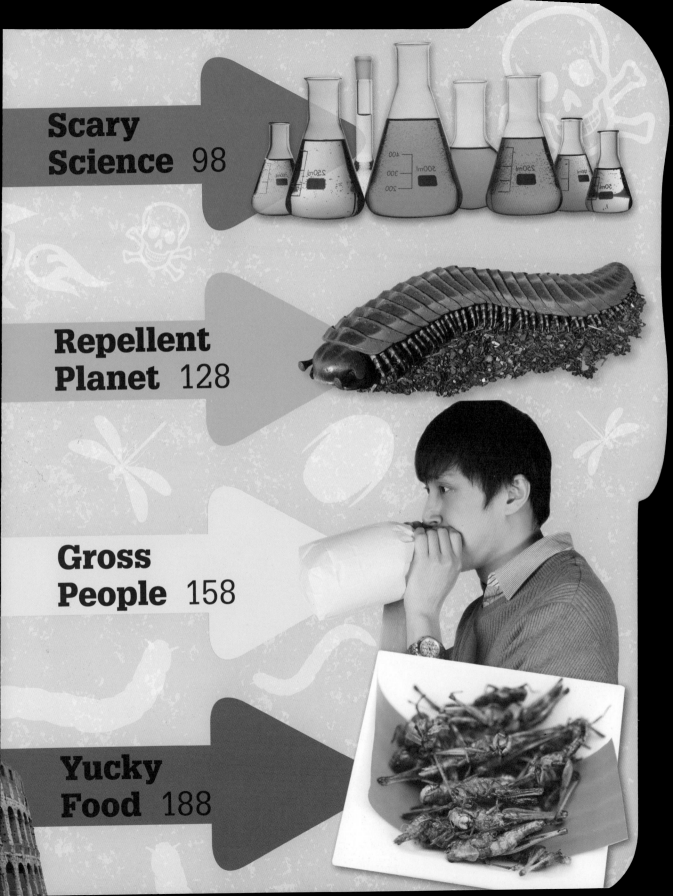

1

BEASTLY

BODIES

Most people have **tiny mites** in their eyelashes, **no matter how clean** they are.

#0001

11 facts about SLIMY SNOT

The scientific word for nose-picking is **RHINOTILLEXOMANIA.**

#0002

A person **swallows about 2 pints of snot** a day without even realizing it.

#0003

Snot is made of **water, salt, and a gluey, sugary substance called mucin** .....

#0004

...When the water dries out it turns into **hard boogers.**

#0005

Snot moves through your breathing tubes at **just over half an inch per hour.** Bamboo grass grows more quickly than this.

#0006

A sneeze hurtles out snot at over 37 MILES PER HOUR— that's nearly twice as fast as a subway train. #0007

The world sneezing record is held by British girl Donna Griffiths. She **SNEEZED A MILLION TIMES IN A ROW.** #0008

If you've been hanging out in a **dusty room,** your snot will be a **GRAY dust-color.** #0009

YOUR SNOT protects you from dirt and germs in the air by catching them. #0011

Your snot looks more **yellow** when you have **a cold** because of all the **white blood cells** in it. #0010

Snot is more than just sticky goo. It contains **antibodies** that help the body recognize **invading bacteria and viruses,** and creates **enzymes** to help kill them. #0012

9 SLOBBERY SPIT FACTS

Your mouth produces between **TWO AND FOUR PINTS OF SPIT** (also known as saliva) a day.

#0013

Your saliva turns your food into a **SOUP-LIKE MIXTURE,** which makes it easier to swallow.

#0015

In some parts of the world, it is thought that a **mother's saliva can help build up a child's immune system**, so moms chew their baby's food before feeding it to them.

#0014

Yawning really hard can make your spit spray **more than a yard.** This is called **GLEEKING.**

#0016

In Singapore, you can be fined **$2,100** for spitting in the street.

#0017

A single COW

makes as much **saliva as 200 HUMANS.** It helps them chew all that grass. #0018

FULMAR CHICKS SPIT

at other animals to keep them away. #0019

Llamas spit when they get annoyed. Their spit is super smelly because it includes food from their stomach. #0020

Spitting cobras spit painful venom **straight into the eyes of predators,** and then slither away to safety. #0021

8 EYE GOO FACTS

Your eyes make tears to wash away dirt and **keep your eyeballs from drying out.** #0022

When you wake up, there is often a **yellow crusty goo** around your eyes. This is **DRIED-OUT TEARS.** #0023

#0024

#0026

Your tears contain water, oil, and mucus (snot!). **This makes the tears stick to your eyes.** #0025

WHEN YOU CRY, **some tears come out of your nose.** They run down a passage connecting your eyes and nose. #0027

You blink about **25 times a minute.** #0028

It takes 100 tears to fill a teaspoon.

If your eye gets an infection or becomes too dry, it may start to leak a yellow, green, or gray fluid known as pus. #0029

4 Icky Earwax Facts

Earwax keeps your ears moist, and makes sure that **dirt** and **bugs** can't get in. #0030

In the 19th century, magazines recommended **using earwax as a lip balm.** #0032

Earwax is made from **sweat, body oil, and dead skin.** #0031

Inside each blue whale's ear is a **foot-long** plug of **earwax,** which protects the eardrum when the whale dives underwater. #0033

7 STOMACH JUICE facts

Fat is hard to digest. It congeals in large globs in your insides, and you need a **substance called bile** to dissolve it. Without the bile, it would just stay there. #0034

The acid in your stomach is strong enough to **eat through metal.** #0035

When stomach acid leaks into your gullet (food pipe), you get a searing feeling called **HEARTBURN.** #0036

Spicy and salty food make your stomach acid even more acidic, which can cause heartburn. #0037

Your body makes more than

14 PINTS
OF DIGESTIVE JUICES

every day. If you tried to drink that much liquid in one go, it would kill you. #0038

Food needs **three to five hours** to dissolve in your stomach juices before it is ready to go to the small intestine. #0039

Your stomach is lined with a gooey mucus that digests the food.

STOMACH ULCERS

happen when there is a gap in the mucus. #0040

3 VILE VOMIT FACTS

Vomit is very **ACIDIC** and **dissolves your teeth.** #0041

Vomit contains half-digested food and bits of stomach lining, which look like **lumps of carrot.** #0042

When one person vomits, it makes **everyone** around them feel sick, too. This can be useful if you've all eaten something **poisonous.** #0043

16

5 PONGY POOP FACTS

Your poop smells because of stinky chemicals called **skatole** and **indole.**

#0044

People fart 14 times a day.

#0045

Cabbage contains **stinky sulfur,** which gives you **smelly farts.**

#0046

1/3 of your **poop** is made of bacteria.

#0047

Corn

passes straight through you, and comes out looking **EXACTLY THE SAME** as when it went in. This is because you cannot digest its tough, fibrous kernels.

#0048

17

11 facts about PEE

When it first comes out, pee is **cleaner** than spit. #0049

urine is 95 percent water. #0050

The other 5 percent is old body cells, unwanted material from your food, and salt. #0051

Ancient Egyptian doctors used to taste people's urine to find out if they were diabetic. #0052

You pee between two and four pints of urine a day. #0053

Some people think **drinking your own pee** makes you healthier. #0054

Throughout your life, you pee about
95,000
pints of urine.

That's enough to fill a small swimming pool. #0055

Your pee is yellow because of a chemical called urochrome. #0056

You can pee faster or slower by controlling the muscles underneath your bladder. #0057

Male lobsters have bladders in their heads, and shoot pee at each other. #0058

If you eat **asparagus,** your pee will smell of it. #0059

5 Facts about Burping

Swallowing air as you eat and drink can make you **BURP and fart.** #0060

Burping gets rid of 2 pt of gas from your **stomach** every day. #0061

Drinking through a straw can **make you burp,** because you swallow more air. #0062

In the zero-gravity of space,
ASTRONAUTS WET BURP because some of their stomach contents come out, too. #0063

The **LOUDEST BURP** ever recorded was as loud as a **car alarm.** #0064

21

8 BAD BACTERIA FACTS

Lots of bacteria live in your armpits and feet. They live off the sweat. #0065

A single ounce of fluid in your large intestine contains 280 trillion bacteria. #0066

There are about 20,000 microbes (tiny bacteria) on every square inch of a desk. #0067

If you could get bacteria to line up in a row, 10,000 would fit across your fingernail. #0069

A piece of chicken that is starting to smell is covered with at least 66 million bacteria per square inch. #0068

Hot water is much better than cold water at getting rid of bacteria from your hands. Most bacteria are frazzled by the heat. #0070

A kitchen sink is home to 10,000 times more germs than a toilet. #0071

One bacterium can turn into millions of bacteria in less than a day. #0072

6 DEADLY DISEASE FACTS

More than 220 million people around the world suffer from malaria each year.

#0073

The Black Death killed more than 25 million people across Europe, which was one third of the population at the time.

#0074

The plague germ was spread by rat fleas. It was called Yersinia pestis.

#0075

On average, one person catches tuberculosis every 3.6 seconds.

#0076

There can be as many as 5 billion viruses in one drop of blood.

#0077

Smallpox killed 30 percent of the people who caught it.

#0078

23

7 SWEATY facts

Sweat is a mixture of water, salt, and minerals that **evaporates into the air,** taking body heat with it.

#0079

If sweat stays on your skin for a while, bacteria start to eat it, creating the pongy chemicals that make you **smell.** #0080

24

Dogs hardly sweat at all, and have to hang out their

TONGUES

to get rid of body heat.

#0081

Hippo sweat is red and sticky, and it acts as

sunblock.
#0082

COWS SWEAT mostly through their noses.

#0084

There are about

250,000

sweat glands on one foot.

#0083

Your feet shed dead skin cells all day. The skin cells mix with **SWEAT** to make a **smelly goo** that is rolled into a **CHEESE** by your toes.

#0085

25

6 FACTS ABOUT BLOOD

The average human has over **10 pt of blood** in their body—enough to fill five family-sized bottles of soda.

#0086

Red blood cells are created and **destroyed** at a rate of about **2 million** per second. That's **173 billion** cells per person per day.

#0087

The amount of blood that is pumped through an average human heart every day would fill about

85 BATHS.

#0088

When you CUT YOURSELF,

16 different **chemicals** work together to turn blood into a **jellylike** clot. After that, a scab can start to form. #0089

PUS

is a gooey yellow goop made from dead **white blood cells** that are left over when your body attacks an **infection.**

#0090

SCABS

start to form less than 10 seconds after a cut has opened.

#0091

15 BRAIN FACTS

Brain surgeons operate on a brain **while the patient is still conscious.**
#0092

Your brain is
80% water.
#0093

While you're awake, your brain is generating **10–23 watts of power.** That's enough to power a lightbulb.
#0097

Everyone has a **unique pattern of wrinkles** on the surface of their brain.
#0094

One fifth of all the oxygen you breathe goes to the **brain.**
#0095

The brain guzzles energy—**it burns 20 percent of your calorie intake,** and uses 15 percent of your blood supply.
#0096

Your brain is highly active when you are asleep. It is busy giving you dreams and nightmares.

#0098

Your brain is busy giving you dreams and nightmares run through electricity through This is called

Doctors sometimes ill patients' brains. Doctors sometimes ill patients send pulses of electricity through their mentally convulsive therapy.

#0099

In ancient Rome, headaches were treated by hitting the patient over the head with **electric fish.**

#0100

In 2007, a 44-year-old Frenchman was found to have a hollow brain. He had lived a totally normal life.

#0101

Special scans called MRI scans track the flow of blood through a live brain, showing which bits are active.

#0102

It is possible to grow human brain cells in a laboratory dish.

#0103

The brain keeps growing until you're about 20, and your personality keeps developing as it grows.

#0104

Brain tissue is the consistency of a soft gelatin dessert.

#0105

Damage to the brain can change your personality, making you kinder or nastier.

#0106

13 Skin and dandruff facts

The skin covering your body is your heaviest organ. Its three layers weigh a hefty **11 pounds.** #0108

A wart is a **KNOBBLY CLUMP** of skin cells that grows when a virus gets into the skin. #0107

People with **Naegeli syndrome** don't have any fingerprints. #0109

If an average person stretched out all their skin, it would be about 22 ft²—**the size of a large bed.** #0110

You shed just under **9 lb of skin each year**—that's about the weight of 40 apples. #0112

Your dead SKIN CELLS

fall off you at a rate of **40,000 a minute.** #0113

One person will shed enough skin in a lifetime to fill a suitcase. #0114

If you collected all the skin shed in one day by the whole world, it would fill a four-story house. #0115

Four out of five teenagers get **acne**—a condition that makes red bumps on your skin. #0111

If your skin is rubbed for too long, it makes a little fluid-filled cushion called a **blister** to protect itself. Beneath the fluid, the skin is safe from friction. #0116

Dandruff

occurs when skin oil glues your dead skin cells into clumps that get trapped by hairs. #0117

Tar has been used to treat dandruff for hundreds of years. #0118

Dandruff can be caused by a fungus in your hair. #0119

14 HAIRY facts

Up to **100 hairs** fall out of your head every day. #0120

YOUR BODY IS COVERED IN HAIR, except the palms of your hands, the soles of your feet, and your lips. #0121

The average head of human hair is strong enough to hold the weight of two adult elephants. #0122

Oil and grease cling to hair, so human hair, along with animal fur, is often used to mop up oil spills. #0123

Fear of bald people is called peladophobia. #0124

A human has the same number of hairs on his or her body as a chimpanzee. #0125

Hair is made from keratin—the same stuff as your fingernails. #0126

The only part of your hair that isn't dead is the bit inside your skin. #0127

TRICHOTILLOMANIA is the urge to pull out, and sometimes even eat, your own hair. #0128

In the 14th century, women in Venice used to dye their hair **blond** with **horse pee.** #0129

In the 18th century, rich people used to wear **WIGS** made from the hair of poor people. #0130

In ancient Rome, pigeon dung was used to dye hair **BLOND.** #0131

The longest beard was grown by Hans Langseth. It was more than 18 ft long—that's the height of three tall men standing on top of each other. #0132

Only 1% of the world's population **have red hair.** In the Middle Ages, redheads were often thought to be witches, werewolves, or vampires! #0133

8 icky facts about babies

A baby's head is three quarters of the size it will be when the child becomes an adult, and a quarter of its total body weight. #0134

Inside the womb, a baby **turns somersaults,** and scratches itself with its fingernails. #0135

Babies are sometimes born with hair all over their heads, back, shoulders, and face, especially if they are born early. #0136

A newborn baby **POOPS** out its own body weight every 60 hours. #0137

Newborn babies have **green poop.** The color is caused by digestive juices that have built up while the baby was in the womb. #0138

A baby will go through nearly
3,000 diapers
a year. #0139

A newborn baby pees every 20 minutes. #0140

One in every
2,000
babies is born
with teeth.
#0141

ABOMINABLE
ANIMALS

Penguins **vomit** food back into their mouths to **feed** **their chicks.**

#0142

8 FARM animal FACTS

A sheep's upper lip is **split in half.** The sheep can move each half separately to choose the best **plant leaves** to eat.

#0143

Male goats **PEE** **on themselves** to attract females.

#0144

PIGS CAN'T SWEAT, so they **roll around in mud** to stay cool.

#0145

A cow's four-chambered stomach releases lots of gas, making it a

CHAMPION FARTER. #0146

A gas called methane, found in **cow manure**, can be used to create **electricity**. #0147

Cows often **stick their tongues up their own noses** to eat the salt and keep flies away. #0148

Humanure is sewage that has been recycled to make **farm fertilizer.** #0149

Newborn foals **eat their mother's poop.** This gives them useful stomach bacteria which help **digest food.** #0150

2 DETESTABLE DOG FACTS

Dogs' noses are about **100,000 times better than humans'.** Some dogs can **smell dead bodies under water** or detect lung cancer by sniffing a person's breath.

#0151

The wetness around a dog's nose is **mucus,** which traps molecules for the dog to sniff. #0152

5 CRAZY CAT FACTS

A cat flea can jump **200 times** its own body length. #0153

Cats **swallow fur** while licking themselves clean, then **vomit it up** as hairballs. #0154

Cats sometimes eat grass to make themselves sick. #0156

Cats mark their territory by pooping around the garden, and even in the house. #0155

Cats kill their prey with a **bite to the neck** that keeps the prey from breathing. #0157

13 facts about vicious HUNTERS

Ghost slugs suck up worms like spaghetti. #0158

Wolverines can take down prey more than **five times bigger** than themselves, killing them with a powerful bite. #0159

To knock insects off low-hanging leaves, the archerfish shoots them with a **well-aimed jet of spit,** then swims over to pick up its meal. #0160

THE PRAYING MANTIS
stabs prey, such as caterpillars, with its spiky legs before eating it. #0161

The Humboldt squid uses suckers on its tentacles to catch fish, then it tears them apart with its beak. #0162

A hyena's bite is so strong that it can crunch through bones. #0163

Ants slice up their prey using their mandibles (jaws) like SCISSORS. #0165

The tentacled water snake makes a splash with the tip of its tail so that frightened fish will swim away, straight into its mouth. #0164

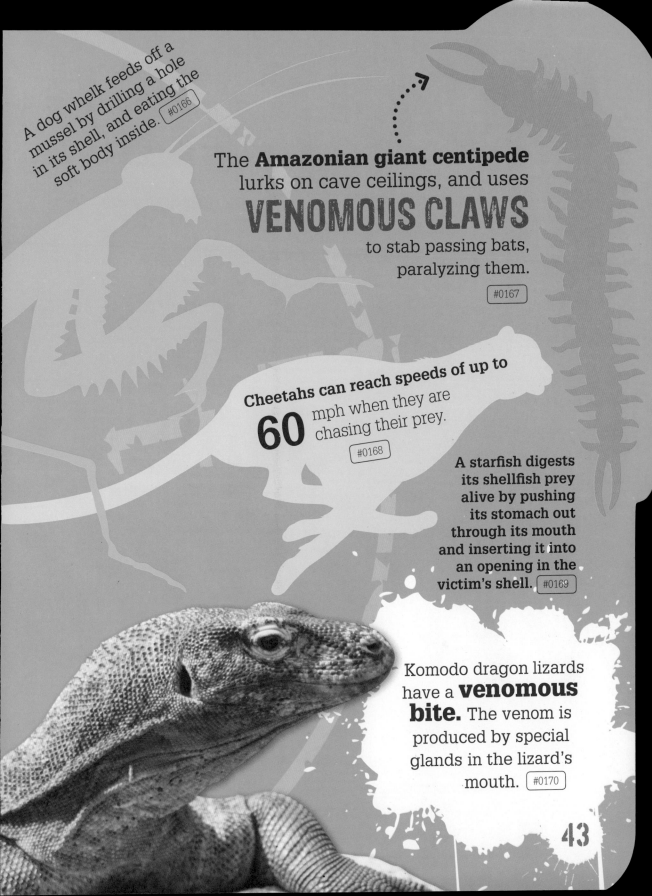

A dog whelk feeds off a mussel by drilling a hole in its shell, and eating the soft body inside. #0166

The **Amazonian giant centipede** lurks on cave ceilings, and uses **VENOMOUS CLAWS** to stab passing bats, paralyzing them.

#0167

Cheetahs can reach speeds of up to **60** mph when they are chasing their prey.

#0168

A starfish digests its shellfish prey alive by pushing its stomach out through its mouth and inserting it into an opening in the victim's shell. #0169

Komodo dragon lizards have a **venomous bite.** The venom is produced by special glands in the lizard's mouth. #0170

10 MAN-EATER facts

Crocodiles often have their mouths open, but it's not because they're hungry, it's because they **sweat through their mouths**. #0171

A Nile crocodile called **GUSTAVE** is thought to have killed **300 PEOPLE.** #0172

Crocodiles and alligators spin their prey around in a "death roll" to kill it. #0173

Wolves have been known to tear at people's throats with their teeth. #0174

Sharks do bite humans, but it is usually by mistake. #0175

Tigers almost always **attack their prey from behind ...** #0176

... So, in India, workers wear masks on the backs of their heads to keep hungry tigers away. #0177

The man-eating Leopard of Rudraprayag killed **more than 125 people** before it was shot in 1926. #0178

Human remains were found in the stomach of a brown bear called Kesagake, who terrorized a Japanese village in 1915. #0179

If you come across a bear, DO NOT turn your back or run away. The bear may see this as weakness, and ATTACK. #0180

11 FACTS ABOUT DEFENSE TACTICS

A deep-sea shrimp escapes danger by shooting out streams of **bioluminescent** glue in the dark, confusing the predator with **blobs** of **light.**

#0181

Sperm whales blast **POOP** into the water as a defense, stirring it up into a brown cloud.

#0184

An **octopus** sends out clouds of **dark ink** to confuse predators.

#0183

The sea cucumber shoots its sticky guts at predators.

#0182

Some starfish **lose limbs** and **regrow** them. A whole **new starfish** can grow from just **one arm.**

#0185

46

Opossums **pretend to be DEAD** if in danger. They lie still for up to four hours, making a vile smell and **leaking green fluid from their bottoms.**

#0186

If a turkey vulture is attacked, it **throws up chunks of meat and vomit** at the face of its attacker. #0187

The skunk uses its **bottom muscles** to shoot out its **stinky spray** over **19 ft.**

#0188

The Iberian ribbed newt can **push its razor sharp ribs outward.** It coats them in runny poison as a double defense.

#0189

Some horned lizards **spout blood** from their **eyes.** The spray can travel up to **12 in.**

#0190

Lots of lizards drop off their tails to confuse attackers. The tail will keep

wriggling

for up to 10 minutes to **distract the enemy** while the lizard escapes. #0191

47

9 POISON AND VENOM facts

The land snake with the most lethal venom is the **Australian inland taipan.**
#0192

The **most potent snake venom** of all comes from a Pacific sea snake, but it is peaceful, and won't attack unless very scared. #0193

In India, **46,000** people die from snake bites a year—that's more than anywhere else in the world.
#0194

Some snake venoms work by shutting down the victim's body so that it is still alive but cannot move. #0195

The **deadly pufferfish** is a delicacy in Japan, and chefs have to take great care to remove the poison. Even so, about 12 people die each year from eating this fish. #0196

The **golden poison frog** has enough deadly poison in it to kill **10 to 20** people. #0197

There are millions of poisonous cane toads in Australia. Dogs sometimes die after licking their toxic skin. #0198

The male **platypus** has venomous spurs on its heels. It uses these to fight other males during the mating season. #0199

Stonefish have **13 venom-filled spines.** #0200

4 FACTS ABOUT
CUCKOO BABIES

Cuckoos lay **their eggs** in **other birds'** nests … #0201

… The cuckoo egg **hatches first,** and **throws** any other **eggs** or **chicks** out of the nest … #0202

… The "parents" do not realize what has happened, and feed the baby cuckoo as if it were their own … #0203

… If the other bird realizes and gets rid of the cuckoo egg, the adult cuckoo will come back and destroy the whole nest. #0204

5 ANIMAL CANNIBAL FACTS

When tadpoles hatch, they will eat any eggs they find nearby, as well as smaller tadpoles.
#0205

Baby caecilians feed by **gnawing off bits of their mother's skin.**
#0206

Adult polar bears, chimps, pigs, hamsters, and wolf spiders have been known to

EAT THEIR OWN BABIES.
#0207

Spider babies of the species *Stegodyphus lineatus* **gobble up their own mother** as their first meal. #0208

The first gray nurse shark babies to hatch from their eggs will **eat their brothers and sisters.** #0209

12 FACTS
ABOUT PESKY
Parasites

The largest parasitic worm ever found

was **28 ft** long. It was found living in a female sperm whale's womb.

#0211

A tapeworm **can live inside a human gut** for up to 20 years. #0212

Tiny **white pinworms** live in your gut, but move to your

BOTTOM

to lay eggs. #0213

Parasitic worm eggs get into soil through animal droppings ... #0214

... There can be **THOUSANDS** of parasitic worm eggs **in one handful of soil**. #0215

Flukes are parasitic worms found in **FISH, CATTLE, AND SHEEP.** Humans can also become infected by swimming in fluke-infested water. #0217

Hookworms can live in your intestine, sucking on **YOUR BLOOD.** #0216

Humans can become infected with the parasite *Toxoplasma gondii* by eating undercooked meat, or coming into contact with **infected cat poop**. #0218

Thorny-headed worms hatch inside pond crustaceans, which are then eaten by ducks. The worm reproduces inside the duck, and its **eggs come out in the duck's poop.** They are then eaten by a crustacean, and the cycle begins again. #0219

A female flea sucks up to **15 TIMES** her own body weight in blood every day.

#0220

The **tongue-eating** louse **EATS THE TONGUE** of its fish victim, and lives in its place. #0221

9 FACTS ABOUT
WEIRD LOOKING ANIMALS

The deep-sea angler lures prey toward its huge mouth using a glowing light at the end of a strange "fishing rod" attached to its head. #0222

WHEN PLAICE ARE BORN ...

... they are shaped like ordinary fish. As they grow, one eye moves around and over the fish's head to be on the same side as the other one.
#0223

DUMBO OCTOPUSES

have floppy fins that look like big ears.
#0224

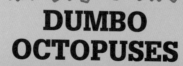

• The nose of the proboscis monkey can stretch out more than 4 in. #0225

The hagfish

produces slime to help it wriggle free from captors. #0226

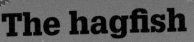

The naked mole rat

is hairless and wrinkled, but it is a tough critter that never gets cancer. #0227

THE BLOBFISH

is a goopy blob with almost no muscle. #0228

The 22 fleshy snouts on a **star-nosed mole** have more than 25,000 touch sensors to help it feel its way underground. #0229

Marabou storks poke their heads into dead bodies to eat. Their heads are bald so they don't get any blood on their feathers. #0230

10 SPIDER FACTS

The female black widow often eats the male after mating. #0231

Poisonous black widows have been found **hiding in bunches of grapes**. #0232

To invade high ground, small spiders can release several threads, which form a **PARACHUTE**. Spiders have been seen as high up as 10,000 ft. #0234

The venomous redback spider of Australia has been known to **lurk beneath toilet seats**. #0233

Ogre-faced spiders weave a web between their front legs. They use the web like a net to catch any prey that flies into it. #0235

The **biggest spider in the world** is the Goliath bird-eating spider, which is as big as a dinner plate.
#0236

Spitting spiders spit a mixture of venom and glue at a victim. This sticks the prey in one place and kills it. #0237

Venomous **Brazilian wandering spiders** can grow up to 5 in wide, and have been found hidden in bunches of bananas.
#0238

The venom of the brown recluse spider is necrotic, meaning it **rots your flesh**.
#0239

Spiders can't digest anything solid. They dissolve food by **injecting digestive juices into their prey**, then they suck up the goop left behind.
#0240

11 facts about WORMS

Lugworms eat **sand,** while earthworms eat **soil.** #0241

A worm is covered in **slimy mucus,** which helps it **absorb oxygen through its skin.** #0242

Earthworms lay their eggs wrapped in a protective cocoon made of **SLIMY MUCUS**. #0243

Earthworms and lugworms **poop wiggly tubes** called worm casts. #0244

Earthworm poop is a great fertilizer for the soil. #0245

The **thousands of tiny hairs** on an earthworm help it grip the soil. #0246

If a worm stays out in the sun for too long, **IT DRIES OUT** and dies. #0247

EARTHWORM BODIES are made up of segments. If a worm loses its back end, it can grow a new one as long as there are enough segments left at the front … #0248

… **The new back end of an earthworm grows back a lighter color.** #0249

The largest worms live in hot countries, and grow up to **10FT** long. #0250

An earthworm is a hermaphrodite, which means it is both male and female. #0251

59

6 Slithery snail Facts

Snails move by **squeezing** and **relaxing** their muscles bit by bit, so they make a **rippling** motion.
#0252

The giant **AFRICAN snail grows** up to

12 in

long and lays an egg **2.5 in** wide.
#0253

As they move, snails create a trail of mucus. The **mucus lubricates the ground,** allowing snails to move more easily.
#0254

Boiled snail pulp was once used to treat burns, and

SNAIL MUCUS

was **smeared on sore skin.**
#0255

Some fish **EAT** water snails by **sucking them out of their shells.**
#0256

Garden snails have over **14,000 teeth** on their radula (tongue).
#0257

4 **Slimy slug** Facts

Most slugs eat **plants,** but **some will hunt down** other slugs by following their **sticky trail.**

#0258

A slug's bottom is on the back of its head.

#0259

SLUG GOOP

has tiny fibers in it that help the slug climb up walls.

#0260

Slugs produce a constant trail of **GOOP** to keep them from **drying out** and dying. #0261

61

8 CREEPY COCKROACH facts

Ancient Greeks used to **grind up cockroaches** into a paste to treat wounds.

#0262

Giant rhino cockroaches are kept as pets by some people. They grow up to

3 in

long, and like to be stroked.

#0263

Cockroaches leave brown POOP marks wherever they go. #0264

Cockroaches sometimes drink moisture from the **MUSTACHES** of sleeping men. #0265

The **tiny hairs** on a cockroach **pick up germs** as they move through drains. #0266

A cockroach can survive for up to a month after losing its head. #0267

A cockroach **sheds its skin** between **10 and 12 times** during its lifetime. #0268

When disturbed, the Florida woods cockroach lets off a foul smell, so it is also known as the **STINKING COCKROACH.** #0269

6 FACTS ABOUT
DEEP-SEA MONSTERS

The **Sloane's viperfish's** teeth are so large that it has to make its jaws vertical to be able to open its mouth wide enough to swallow its prey. #0270

The **giant squid** has a hard beak, shaped like a parrot's. Scientists believe the squid uses it to dismember or paralyze its prey. #0271

Gulper eels are almost all mouth and no body—they have giant hinged mouths, and can eat animals much larger than themselves. #0272

Flashlight fish have luminous bacteria behind their retinas, giving them glowing eyes, which they can blink on to attract prey, or off to avoid predators. #0274

The goblin shark looks for food with its snout. It catches prey with a jaw that can reach right out of its mouth. #0273

Zombie worms dissolve holes in whale bones, then live inside the bones. #0275

10 FACTS ABOUT
BUGS in the home

The **house centipede kills prey** by **injecting venom** with its fangs.
#0276

A daddy longlegs spider **catches its prey by weaving a cocoon**, rendering its victim helpless.
#0277

Bed bugs are flat, button-shaped parasites that **live in mattresses** and **drink your blood** at night.
#0278

Carpet beetle larvae are also known as **WOOLLY BEARS** because they **love to eat natural fibers** found in items such as carpets, curtains, and clothes.
#0279

The **colossus earwig** grows up to **2.5 in long.**
#0280

Earwigs come out at night, eating other insects, eggs, and even each other.
#0281

You shed enough flakes of skin in one day to feed **one million dust mites.**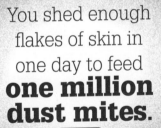

#0282

Between two and **three million dust mites live in the average bed** mattress.

#0283

Dust mites only live for a couple of months ... #0284

... But during that time they produce up to

200 **times their own body weight in POOP.** #0285

HIDEOUS
HISTORY

The Vikings believed that the first people came from the **sweat** of a **mythical creature**, the **earth** from his **flesh**, the **hills** from his **bones**, and the **oceans** from his **blood.** #0286

6 STONE AGE LIFE facts

Cave paintings were made **30,000** years ago using paint made from dirt or charcoal mixed with spit, animal fat, or urine. #0287

In 1950, Tollund Man, a **2,500-year-old** corpse, was found **naturally mummified in a peat bog.** #0288

Ancient human skulls from

160,000 years ago

have been found with cut marks in them, suggesting **CANNIBALISM**.

#0289

Stone Age people stitched up wounds using **needles made of bone,** and **thread made of muscle tissue.** #0290

In 1991, the **5,000-year-old** body of a hunter nicknamed Ötzi was found **perfectly preserved in ice** in the Alps, Europe. #0291

During the last
ICE AGE

people built houses using **mammoth bones** as struts. #0292

71

12 ANCIENT ROMAN FACTS

Roman fortune tellers would **predict the future** by studying the guts of **sacrificed animals.**
#0293

It was considered polite **to belch** in ancient Rome.
#0297

PUBLIC TOILETS

were a **line of holes** in a long stone seat with running water below to flush the waste away. #0294

Men would go to public toilets to be social and **have a chat.** #0295

Romans wiped their bums with **a sponge on a stick.** #0296

Romans cleaned their clothes **with pee.**
#0298

People visited the Colosseum in Rome to watch gladiators fight. Sometimes the crowds called for the loser to be killed. #0299

After a death in the arena, a referee would hit the corpse over the head with a mallet, to show that it now belonged to Pluto, god of the underworld. #0300

In lunch intervals at the Colosseum, criminals were thrown into a no-win fight with **hungry lions and tigers.** #0301

Drinking gladiator BLOOD was recommended by Roman doctors to treat epilepsy. #0302

Ostrich brains were a delicacy in ancient Rome. #0303

Roman fathers were shown their newborn babies and could decide whether they lived or died. #0304

17
facts about AZTECS

Aztec Emperor Tlacaelel started a **war** so that he could **gather more prisoners to sacrifice** to the gods. #0305

Only wealthy Aztecs were allowed to wear feathers. #0306

The Aztecs used **cocoa beans** as money. #0307

Priests would cut themselves ... #0308 spill the blood onto paper ... #0309 and burn it as an offering to the gods. #0310

If a person died, sometimes the Aztecs would also kill a dog and bury it with the person, **so that it could guide them on their journey through the afterlife.** #0311

It was not uncommon for someone who was poor to **sell their own children into slavery** ... #0312

... Many Aztecs would also sell *themselves* into slavery ... #0313

... Some remained slaves most of their lives. #0314

Aztecs played a ball game called **Ulamaliztli**. The ball was said to represent the head of a **sacrificed victim.** #0315

The losing team would then be **sacrificed.** #0316

Doctors in ancient Mexico treated earache by pouring **hot liquid rubber** into the ear. #0317

Poor Aztecs would eat a scum made of algae, known as **"stone dung."** #0318

An annual ritual to the

RAIN GOD,

Tlaloc, involved making a child cry. #0319

Smallpox killed 3 million Aztecs when the Spanish brought the disease to Mexico. #0320

Ruler Moctezuma II was **killed by his own people** for surrendering to the Spaniards. #0321

75

9 facts about
EGYPTIAN MUMMIES

It took 70 days for the ancient Egyptians to make a mummy out of a dead body. #0322

First, they cut open the body with a **sharp stone**, then removed the **stomach, lungs, and other organs,** and put them in **jars** near the body. #0323

The HEART was left inside the body. It was thought to be vital for the AFTERLIFE. #0324

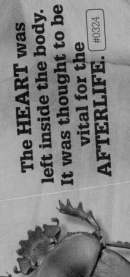

A sacred **scarab beetle** was placed on the heart. #0325

Using a hammer and chisel, they knocked a **hole** into the nose bone and hooked out the **brain**. #0326

The Egyptians thought the brain was unimportant, and threw it away. #0327

Then they stuffed the body with **bandages** and **sawdust,** covered it completely with salt, and left it for a month to dry out. #0328

After the month, they wrapped the mummy in RESIN-SOAKED BANDAGES while casting spells over it. #0329

Pharaoh Tutankhamun's mummy shows that he may have **died from gangrene** (a stinking flesh-rotting infection) after he broke his leg. #0330

11 Facts about
CASTLES

Medieval soldiers attacking a castle would hurl

DEAD ANIMALS

and **human heads** at it from giant wooden catapults ... #0331

... The rotting corpses would **spread disease** inside the castle. #0332

Lords would **cut off a criminal's head, and stick it on a pole** above the castle's portcullis (entrance) as a warning to others. #0333

CATS AND DOGS

were kept to **kill the rats** that would eat the castle's food supply. #0334

Castle guests would leave their coats in the **"garderobe"**, which was **inside the castle toilet.** They thought the stink protected the clothes from fleas. #0335

Castle floors were covered in straw. Mixed in with the straw could be **grease, bones, spit, and even dog poop.** #0336

People would **poop out of holes** in a castle's wall. #0337

Murder-holes were put in the ceilings of a passageway so defenders could **pour burning oil** onto attackers. #0338

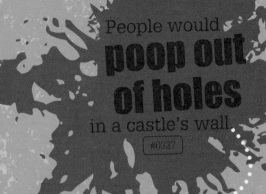

Workers called **gong farmers** had to clean up the mess. #0339

Prisoners were often thrown into deep holes called

oubliettes.

The name means "forgotten place" in French, and prisoners were often left there to die. #0340

In 1203, Phillip II's soldiers surrounded Château Gaillard in Normandy, France. They broke into the castle by **crawling through a sewage trench**. #0341

11 Perilous *Pirate* facts

The worst pirates were **hanged,** and their bodies were **covered in tar** and left to **rot publicly** in an iron cage. #0342

After **William Kidd** was caught in 1701, his corpse was left to rot for **three years.** #0343

Pirates would collect fresh food when they landed, but on ship it quickly went **stale or moldy.** Not eating enough good food often made pirates sick—their **teeth fell out** and their **skin went pale**. #0344

Henry Morgan accidentally blew up his own ship, killing 350 men. #0345

Edward Teach was also known as **Blackbeard**. When he attacked a ship, he'd tie lit **gunpowder** fuses into his beard to scare his victims. #0346

Edward Teach liked to drink **rum** mixed with **gunpowder**. #0347

Pirate flags were designed to **terrify people,** sending the message **"surrender quickly or die."** #0348

MINOR OFFENSES were punished by flogging pirates with a knotted rope. #0349

As punishment, a pirate might be dragged on a rope under the ship ... #0350

... He would either drown or be slashed by the razor-sharp barnacles on the ship's hull. #0351

A cheating fellow pirate would be left on a desert island with a little food, water, and a **loaded pistol** to kill himself. #0352

12 facts about Crazy Royals

English King Henry II had a jester called Roland the Farter, who would **fart on demand.**
#0354

English King Henry VIII had a groom of the stool— a man who **wiped his bottom** for him. #0353

To keep guests entertained at a feast, Roman Emperor Caligula would **behead** criminals in between courses. #0355

When his sister died, Caligula was so upset **he banned people from laughing, on pain of DEATH**. He also banned them from taking a bath. #0356

Louis XIV of France only took **three baths** in his lifetime. #0357

In 1762, Korean Prince Sado was **locked in a rice chest** by his father. He died after eight days. #0358

King Nabonidus of Babylon thought he was a **goat,** and insisted on **grazing in a field.** #0359

Duke Gian Gastone of Tuscany, Italy, **stayed in a stinking bed for 7 years,** refusing to get up. #0360

By the time he died, aged 55, Henry VIII was **covered in boils** and so **overweight** that he couldn't move about by himself. #0361

Don Carlos, son of Spanish King Phillip II, forced a shoemaker to **eat a pair of shoes** that weren't up to standard. #0362

Anna of Russia built an **ICE PALACE** to celebrate the marriage of a prince she did not like. She made the married couple stay there on their wedding night. #0363

When they had finished building St. Basil's Cathedral in Moscow, Russian Tsar Ivan the Terrible had the designers **blinded,** so they could never build anything better. #0364

83

7 Bad medicine facts

In ancient Egypt, rubbing your eyes with **mashed tortoise brains** was a treatment for bad eyesight. #0365

Egyptian doctors recommended **treating toothache** by holding a **freshly killed mouse** on your gums. #0366

For centuries, Europeans thought the world was made of four kinds of things, called **"humours,"** which were represented in the body by:

```
yellow          blood
bile

black           phlegm
bile
```

#0367

In the Middle Ages, doctors treated many illnesses with **bloodletting** —taking some of the patient's blood. It usually just made the patient **even weaker.** #0368

An ancient surgery called **trepanning** involved **drilling a hole** in the patient's skull. #0369

One attempted **cure for the plague** involved **strapping a plucked chicken to your body.** #0370

To make **rotten teeth fall out,** Tudor dentists used a mixture of **poop and honey.** #0371

85

9 Freaky facts about Fashion

In Europe in the 1100s, shoes with **very long, curly toes** were fashionable. They were called **"pikases"** because they had a pointed end, like a pike.

#0372

Before the 19th century, there was no such thing as a fashion model. Instead, designers used **little dolls** to show their fashions to customers.

#0373

In the 1600s, fashionable men and women wore **white makeup** made of **LEAD**. The lead was poisonous, and rotted their skin.

#0374

In the 17th century, Louis XIII of France wanted to hide his baldness so he began a fashion for the periwig, a lavish wig for men. **A bigger wig made the wearer more fashionable.**

#0375

In 17th century France, the bleach used to color clothes was made from **URINE**. #0376

French leader Napoleon Bonaparte first added buttons to jacket sleeves. He wanted to keep soldiers from **wiping their runny noses** on their sleeves. #0377

Aristocrats in Tibet wore sleeves so long that their hands were hidden. It showed that they were **above** doing manual work. #0378

In the 1880s, many women wore **bustles** under their dresses. These were frames or pads designed to **make their bottoms look huge**. #0379

Many Chinese women were **crippled by the fashion for tiny feet.** Young girls' toes were **broken** and wrapped tightly in bandages to keep their feet from growing. #0380

7 CHILDREN AT WORK FACTS

Young crossing sweepers would clear the streets of **litter** and **horse poop** so that rich people wouldn't get their clothes dirty. #0381

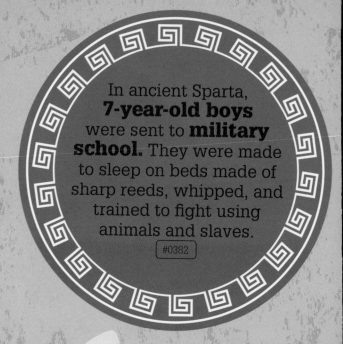

In ancient Sparta, **7-year-old boys** were sent to **military school.** They were made to sleep on beds made of sharp reeds, whipped, and trained to fight using animals and slaves. #0382

Kids in the 1800s collected **dog and cat poop.** The poop was used to soften leather before it could be made into clothes and bags. #0383

In coal mines, trucks full of coal were pushed along narrow tunnels by children. #0384

In 19th-century Europe, matches were made by girls using **poisonous phosphorus.** #0385

Some children in mines would stay underground up to **18 hours** a day. #0386

Because they were **small enough** to fit up chimneys, Victorian children were sent up flues to **sweep them out.** #0387

7 FACTS ABOUT FILTHY FACTORIES

Men who live near the weapons factory in Dzerzinsk, Russia, **die at an average age of 42** due to the water pollution.

#0388

A chemical factory in Ranipet, India, has made a pile of toxic waste that weighs **1.5 million tons.**

#0389

Slag heaps are large mounds of waste that are piled up around mining towns. In the past these heaps have **collapsed,** creating dangerous landslides.

#0390

A spill from a pesticide factory in Bhopal, India, created a toxic cloud that killed up to 20,000 people.
#0391

When car-manufacturer Henry Ford visited a slaughterhouse, he saw the dead cows hanging in a line, and how quickly they were processed. After this visit, he came up with the idea of using an "assembly line" in his factories.
#0392

Luddites were people who protested against the rise of factories by **smashing machines** and attacking merchants.
#0393

Women working in British arms factories during World War I were nicknamed "canaries" because their skin was stained yellow by the sulfur used to make weapons.
#0394

12 DREADFUL DESPOTS FACTS

Turkish Sultan Abdul Assiz was so **scared of intruders** that he had his palace **rigged** with **booby traps** and **hidden guns** triggered by wires. #0395

Maximilien Robespierre was a leader of the **French Revolution.** He sent his enemies to the **guillotine,** but in the end was guillotined himself. #0396

In 1893, American James Harden-Hickey claimed an Atlantic island, declared himself **King James I,** and printed his **own money.** #0397

Ivan the Terrible, the 16th-century Russian Tsar, once dressed an archbishop in **bear furs** and then had him hunted to death by a pack of **ferocious dogs.** #0398

Turkmenistan's dictator Saparmurat Niyazov banned **ballet, opera,** and the **circus** in 2001, and forbade men to **have beards** or **long hair** in 2004. #0399

While his people **went hungry,** North Korean despot Kim Jong-il had delicious treats **flown to him** from all over the world. #0400

Romanian dictator Nicolae Ceausescu had a henchman to **disinfect his palms** every time he **shook hands** with someone. #0401

Kim also made servants **check every single grain of rice** to ensure it was the highest quality before it ended up on his plate. #0402

VLAD THE IMPALER
dined among the impaled corpses of his victims. #0403

Egyptian pharaoh Pepi II had slaves covered in

HONEY.

The slaves would stand next to the pharaoh and **draw flies away** from him. #0404

German dictator Adolf Hitler's vegetarian diet gave him **uncontrollable farting.** #0405

When Libyan tyrant Muammar Gaddafi **travelled abroad,** he needed **four jet airliners** to transport his troop of female bodyguards, his camels, and his tent. #0406

10 FACTS ABOUT INTREPID EXPLORERS

Polar explorers used to **eat their sled dogs** during the course of an expedition.
#0407

British explorer Ranulph Fiennes **sawed off his own fingers** that had been damaged by frostbite.
#0408

Some of the **health effects** of long polar trips include **NAUSEA, DIZZINESS, HAIR AND NAIL LOSS, AND EYES AND SKIN GOING YELLOW.**
#0409

Swiss Antarctic explorer Xavier Mertz died after eating too much **dog liver.** He was poisoned by the high level of vitamin A.
#0410

In 1819, British explorer John Franklin led an expedition in which 11 of the 20 explorers died. In 1845, he led an expedition to the Arctic, and the **whole crew died.**
#0411

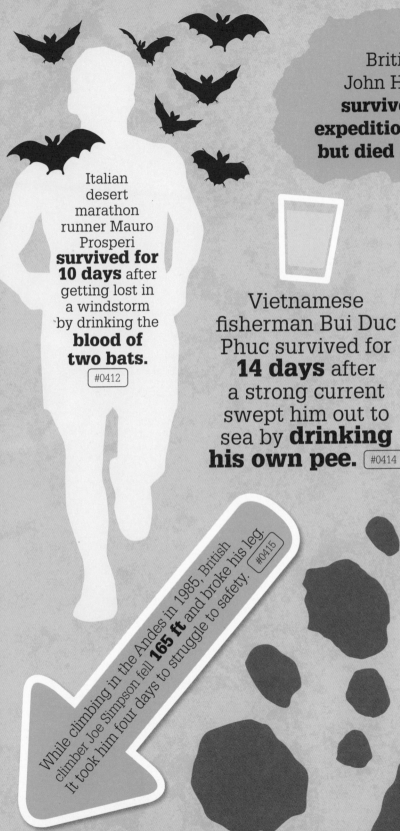

Italian desert marathon runner Mauro Prosperi **survived for 10 days** after getting lost in a windstorm by drinking the **blood of two bats.**

#0412

British explorer John Hanning Speke **survived dangerous expeditions** around Africa, **but died** after accidentally **shooting himself** while at home in England.

#0413

Vietnamese fisherman Bui Duc Phuc survived for **14 days** after a strong current swept him out to sea by **drinking his own pee.**

#0414

While climbing in the Andes in 1985, British climber Joe Simpson fell **165 ft** and broke his leg. It took him four days to struggle to safety.

#0415

When a huge boulder fell on explorer **Aron Ralston** in Utah in 2003, he had to **cut off his trapped hand with a penknife** to escape.

#0416

95

11 facts about Crazy Artists

After a fight with fellow artist Gauguin, Vincent van Gogh **cut off his own ear.** #0417

The poet Tennyson liked to do an impression of a man sitting on the toilet. #0418

The poet Swinburne once slid down the banister naked at a dinner party. #0419

Romantic poet Lord Byron lived with a variety of pets, including a crocodile, a goat, and a heron. #0420

Surrealist artist Marcel Duchamp made a piece called *Fountain*, which was nothing more than a urinal. #0421

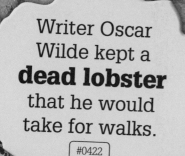

Writer Oscar Wilde kept a **dead lobster** that he would take for walks.
#0422

Performance artist Chris Burden once nailed himself to a car.
#0423

A Belgian artist made a sculpture using **8,000 slices of ham.** As the meat began to stink, it attracted swarms of flies, turning it into "living sculpture."
#0424

The artist Salvador Dalí was afraid of grasshoppers— when they appear in his work, they are used as a symbol of destruction, waste, and fear.
#0425

Artist Marc Quinn made a frozen sculpture of his head from 9.5 pt of his **own blood.**
#0426

Artist Damien Hirst pickled a large tiger shark in formaldehyde, and put it on show in a tank.
#0427

4 SCARY SCIENCE

Scientists believe they might be able to restore the sight of blind people by studying the **eyes** of insects. They believe they can copy the compound eyes to replicate

"INSECT-VISION."

#0428

11 MAD SCIENTIST facts

Dutch scientist Antoni van Leeuwenhoek **discovered bacteria** by studying the **plaque on his own teeth** under a microscope. #0429

Inventor Leonardo da Vinci cut up **dead horses and humans** to learn how their bodies worked. #0430

In 1796, English scientist Edward Jenner **deliberately infected an 8-year-old** boy with a mild disease called **cowpox.** He found that the boy became immune to **deadly smallpox** and he was able to create a **vaccine** against the terrible disease that saved millions of lives. #0431

British physicist Sir Isaac Newton was believed to have had a **mental breakdown** in 1692. However, his strange behavior is now thought to have been caused by **mercury poisoning.** #0432

In the 18th century, Johann Konrad Dippel invented an oil that he thought would help people to **live forever.** However, it was only useful as an animal repellent and a poison. #0433

100

In the 18th century, Italian scientist Luigi Galvani made a **dead frog's legs twitch** using

electricity.

This made him think he could use electricity to bring the dead back to life. #0434

When Christian Schönbein mopped up acid with his wife's cotton apron, it caused the apron to explode. He had discovered nitrocellulose or **"guncotton."** #0435

In the 18th century, U.S. doctor Stubbins Ffirth tested how **yellow fever** might be spread by drinking

INFECTED VOMIT.

His theories were wrong, however, because yellow fever is spread by mosquitoes. #0436

As well as helping develop the electrical supply you use today, Nikola Tesla also claimed to have invented a **"death ray" weapon,** an **earthquake machine,** and a method for **splitting the world in two.** #0437

In the early 19th century, Andrew Ure, a Scottish doctor, tried to bring a **hanged man back to life by sending an electric current through his neck.** #0438

Ilya Ivanovich Ivanov tried to create a **HUMANZEE** (a human-chimpanzee hybrid) in 1927. #0439

8 foul facts about INVENTIONS

In the early 1900s, scientist **Marie Curie** discovered the radioactive elements **polonium and radium,** but she fell ill after carrying tubes containing the **dangerous** **chemicals in her pockets.**

#0440

In 1867, William Bullock developed **gangrene** and died after crushing his foot in **his own invention**—the rotary printing press. #0441

The toilet snorkel was invented in 1982 to provide **clean air via the toilet bowl, in case of fire.** #0442

In 1995, the babyvac

was invented to **clean snot out of babies' noses** so that they could breathe more easily. #0443

102

In 2005, scientists in Singapore created a battery powered by **URINE.**

#0444

In 1908, George Hogan designed an alarm clock that **tipped water onto a sleeping person** to wake them up.

#0445

The Aspire Assist Aspiration Therapy System was invented in 2013. It is a **weight-loss device** that pumps food out of your stomach before your body can digest it.

#0446

Scientists in Japan have invented a **FART RECORDER** that **analyzes a fart's smell** and then recreates it using a mixture of chemicals.

#0447

9 more vile INVENTIONS

In 2009, designer Mike Thomson invented a **lamp that needs a** **DROP OF BLOOD** **to make it work.** He hoped it would make people think twice before turning on the lamp!

#0448

In 2008, New York unveiled its first **automated pay toilet.** The user has a **15-minute time limit,** after which the door flies open.

#0449

The White Goat machine can recycle used office paper into toilet paper in about **30 minutes.** Unfortunately, the machine is the size of **two closets.**

#0450

The Bird Trap and Cat Feeder was a fake birdhouse that lured birds in and then trapped them. Cats could then come along and eat the caged bird. #0451

Hair-in-a-Can

was meant to be spray-on hair to cover bald patches. It looked so bad that most people preferred being bald.

#0452

Thomas Midgley Jr.'s inventions have caused a lot of **damage to the environment.** As well as **leaded petrol,** he developed **CFCs**. These are the gases that were found in **refrigerators and aerosols** and created a huge hole in the **ozone layer.**

#0453

American scientists are developing a **3D food** printer, which will allow you to "print off" edible food, using raw food as **"ink."**

#0454

SMELL-O-VISION

was an invention to **release scent** during a movie. It was used briefly in the 1960s, but was so unpopular that it has **not been attempted since.** #0455

Moviemakers are working on a **"touch jacket"** that will make your skin crawl and send shivers up your spine while you watch a movie. #0456

11 FACTS ABOUT EXPERIMENTS

In 1928, while trying to perfect blood transfusion, Russian scientist Alexander Bogdanov fatally **injected himself** with infected blood.

#0457

In 1964, Australian doctor Jack Barnes allowed himself and his 9-year-old son to be **stung by a jellyfish** and proved that it was the cause of the dangerous **Irukandji syndrome.**

#0458

During the Cold War, the CIA fitted a **spy cat** with hidden microphones. Unfortunately, a taxi crushed it on its first test run.

#0461

During World War II, the U.S. tried attaching bombs to bats. However, some of the bats roosted under a fuel tanker and set fire to a U.S. air base.

#0459

In 2004, scientists at the University of Washington received **poop by mail** because park rangers in Africa sent them elephant dung to analyse the DNA. The scientists created a **poop-inspired map of the elephant population** across Africa.

#0460

In 1997, American scientists **grew a human-shaped ear on the back of a mouse.** #0465

Giovanni Grassi ate **roundworm eggs** to prove how the parasites are transmitted. He found that the eggs **passed through his body** and hatched in his **own poop.** #0463

To find out how humans could live alone in space, French geologist Michel Siffre lived inside an **underground glacier** with no daylight for two months. #0464

In 1938, John Deering volunteered to be monitored **during his execution** so that doctors could learn what happened to the body during death by gunshot. #0467

In 1942, Professor Lawrence Leshant conducted a sleep-learning experiment on boys at a summer camp who were diagnosed as chronic nail-biters. Every night, while they slept, he played a repeat message: **"My fingernails taste terribly bitter."** By the end of the summer, 40 percent had kicked the habit. #0462

In 1901, Ivan Pavlov observed that dogs salivated when they were given food, so he rang a bell at the same time. Soon, he was able to make the dogs drool just by ringing the bell, even if there was **no food.** #0466

107

7 facts about STINKY SCIENCE

At the end of the 20th century, American chemists developed the **world's worst smell,** a foul mixture known as **STENCH SOUP.**

#0468

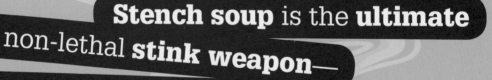

Stench soup is the **ultimate** non-lethal **stink weapon**— anyone who smells it will run away in the opposite direction.

#0469

Hydrogen sulfide, a common chemical compound, is both **dangerous** and **disgusting**. It is POISONOUS, FLAMMABLE, EXPLOSIVE— and it smells of **ROTTEN EGGS.**

#0470

108

AMMONIA

can be found in FERTILIZERS, CLEANING PRODUCTS, HUMAN KIDNEYS, and on ripe cheeses such as CAMEMBERT. Unfortunately, it smells like **URINE!** #0471

A SMELLY SUBSTANCE called **Standard Bathroom Malodor** is used to test deodorizers and air fresheners. It smells like **human poop**, only much stronger. #0472

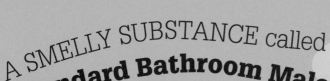

Farms are smelly because the gases from the **animals' farts** and **poop** mix with dust particles in the air. #0473

A **dirty dishcloth** smells really **bad**, thanks to the millions of **YUCKY BACTERIA** growing on it. #0474

9 facts about
CHEMICALS

DDT (dichloro-diheyl-trichloreoethene) was a popular insecticide, until it was found to poison birds and marine organisms, and affect human health. #0475

All of the **oxygen** you breathe on Earth is a plant waste product. #0476

In small doses, **nitroglycerin** can be used in heart medication. In large doses, it is used in explosives. #0477

Sodium phosphate can be used as a food additive—it is also used in soap. #0478

Propylene glycol is found in lime- or orange-flavored foods and animal feed, but it is also found in antifreeze and **can be used to poison beetles.** #0479

While **fluoride** helps prevent tooth decay, **hydrofluoric acid** is so corrosive that it will dissolve glass. #0480

Titanium dioxide, used as food coloring in salad dressings, is also used in sunscreen and paint. #0481

Some lipsticks contain **lead**. This makes the lipstick mildly toxic—but only if it is eaten. #0482

The hardest substance in your body is in your tooth enamel. #0483

10 facts about BIOLOGY

The BROWN MARMORATED STINK BUG releases a **FOUL-SMELLING ODOR** from holes in its abdomen.

#0484

On an average day, you will **inhale** about 2 pt of other people's FART GASES.

#0485

The **Rafflesia arnoldii** is the largest flower on Earth. It attracts flies to pollinate it by producing a **stink** like **rotting meat**.

#0486

The **bird-dropping spider** has developed a **foolproof disguise** to avoid predators— it looks **exactly** like **bird poop!**

#0487

When you **blush**, your **stomach lining** turns **red**. #0488

There are more tiny organisms on the skin of one human than there are human beings on Earth. #0489

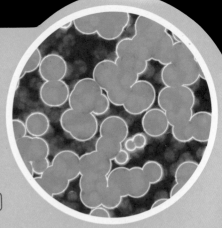

The **TURKEY VULTURE** scares off predators by VOMITING FOUL-SMELLING, SEMIDIGESTED food. #0490

The turkey vulture also uses its own **poop** to cool its body. #0491

The **human body** contains enough **fat** to produce **seven bars of soap**. #0492

The tiny **GOLDEN DART FROG** is one of the most poisonous creatures in the world. Its skin is coated with **enough poison** to kill up to

20 HUMANS. #0493

12 facts about SURGERY

ANCIENT ROMANS
practiced plastic surgery to repair
noses, **eyes**, **lips**, and **teeth**.

#0494

One procedure in **ancient Rome** was
the removal of **scar tissue** from the
back, because it implied that a man had
turned his back in battle and was a

COWARD.

#0495

Most surgeries in
Renaissance times
(14th–17th centuries)
were performed in
BARBERSHOPS.

#0496

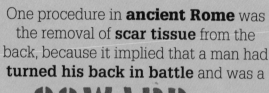

Many of the patients seen by
16th-century Italian surgeon
GASPARE TAGLIACOZZI
were treated for wounds caused by
DUELS or **STREET FIGHTS.**

#0497

Tagliacozzi created **new
noses** using **ARM TISSUE.**
However, the new nose could
fall off if the person
blew it too hard.

#0498

Australian artist Stelios Arcadious had an **EAR** grown from cells in a laboratory implanted in his arm to make him a living art exhibit. #0499

About **17 million** plastic surgery operations are carried out every year worldwide … #0500

… More take place in SWITZERLAND than any other country, with about **216 procedures** per **100,000 people** each year. #0501

In the Middle Ages, surgeons used **herbs** and **alcohol** as simple anesthetics. #0502

The earliest form of surgery was **trepanning,** which involved cutting a small round hole in the head. #0503

In 2007, a man in Colorado had his **THUMBS NARROWED** so that he could **use his iPhone more efficiently.** #0504

Some fashion-conscious women have a **toe bone removed** so that they can wear slim-fitting shoes. #0505

115

14 facts about GENETICS

To save time on sheep shearing, Australian scientists developed a sheep whose **wool drops out** after it has reached a certain length.
#0506

In 1985, scientists developed **a pig** that grew so big it became crippled with arthritis.
#0507

Scientists have created a **POISONOUS CABBAGE**. Any hungry caterpillar that tries to eat it will **drop dead.** Luckily, the cabbage is harmless to humans!
#0508

To protect potato crops, scientists in the 1990s developed potato plants that would **die** if they became **infected by diseases or parasites.**
#0509

Phosphorus found in pig poop can cause environmental damage, so scientists developed **"Enviropig,"** a pig that produces less phosphorus in its poop.
#0510

The **Tasmanian tiger** became extinct in the 1930s but scientists have **used remains** from a specimen to try and recreate tiny cells.
#0511

Mercury is a **poisonous metal.** In the early 21st century, American scientists developed **poplar trees** that could suck up mercury from contaminated soil through their roots.

#0512

British scientists have produced a **breed of hen** that lays eggs with cancer-fighting properties.

#0513

In 1993, scientists developed **goats** that could produce a **spider silk** protein in their milk. They used these animals to manufacture a very strong material called **biosteel.**

#0515

In 1951, scientists discovered that cells taken from cancer patient **Henrietta Lacks** could be kept alive and made to multiply. They were named HeLa ...

#0514

... HeLa cells have been used for research into **cancer, AIDS,** toxic substances, and many other areas.

#0516

Trees are being genetically altered to grow faster and withstand biological attacks.

#0517

Scientists have developed **bananas** that can carry vaccines. Instead of having an injection, you just eat a banana to protect yourself from diseases.

#0518

Cow farts are a major contributor to global warming. So scientists in America have bred a cow that farts **25 percent less** than normal cows.

#0519

5 filthy facts about the VIRTUAL WORLD

There are more devices connected to the Internet than there are **people on the entire planet.** #0520

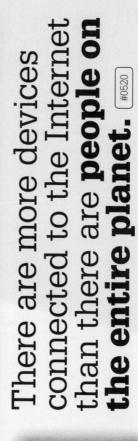

Of the 6 billion people living on Earth in 2012, 4.8 billion had a cell phone but only **4.2 billion owned a toothbrush.** #0521

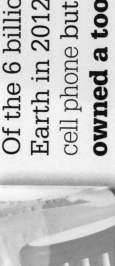

400 million people around the world play **MMO** (Massively Multiplayer Online) video games, spending $13 billion in 2012, more than the U.S. spends on **cosmetics in a year**. #0522

In total, gamers have spent the equivalent of **200,000 years** playing **Angry Birds**, approximately the same amount of time that **humans have existed**. #0523

More than half of smartphone owners check their Facebook page before they get **out of bed** in the morning, and one third will read it **on the toilet.** #0524

8 gross computer facts

SPIDER infestations, **mice, cockroaches,** and even **dead lizards** have been found inside home PCs. #0525

It takes **495 lb** of **fossil fuel, 49 lb** of **chemicals**, and **1.5 tons** of **water** to manufacture **one computer**. #0526

DRY EYES ARE A COMMON PROBLEM for computer users because the average person only blinks **7 TIMES PER MINUTE** when using a computer, less than half the normal amount. #0527

120

An estimated
50 million tons of

W.E.E.E.

(Waste Electrical and
Electronic Equipment) are
produced each year—that's
the equivalent of **100 fully
laden oil tankers.**

#0528

Computers are getting smaller,
more powerful, and more portable.
Google has made a **wearable**
computer, in the form of
voice-activated **glasses.** #0529

An average 21-year-old has spent
**5,000 hours playing
video games.** They have
also sent 250,000 emails, instant
messages, and texts, spent 10,000
hours on a mobile phone,
and picked their nose
30,000 times.

#0530

SINCE 1997,
it has been possible to have a
computer **implanted in your
brain** to help control neural
diseases, such as **epilepsy.**

#0531

100 million
phones are disposed of in
Europe **each year**—that's more
than the **combined populations**
of Germany and Romania.

#0532

121

11 CRAZY ROBOT FACTS

First released in 2004, the **"robosapien"** was a toy robot that was built to behave like a human, even making **farting and belching sounds.**
#0533

In 2005, a U.K. scientist began developing an **Ecobot** that will be powered by **bacteria from rotting apples and dead flies.**
#0536

Kobe Airport in Japan has a robot called **DCBA** that can clean a urinal in 10 seconds. #0534

A **robot toilet** at Frankfurt Airport in Germany has its own arm that **sprays water** at the toilet bowl to clean it. #0535

In his 2000 book *Robot*, Hans Moravec predicts that robots will be able to match human intelligence by 2040 and by 2050 they will be smarter.
#0537

Since 2000, the da Vinci robotic surgical system has been **helping surgeons** perform minor operations.
#0538

The Mondo Spider is a 1,600-lb, 8-legged, solar-powered **walking machine** originally built in 2006.
#0539

Developed in 2012, **Kenji the robot** was programmed to **fall in "love."** Unfortunately Kenji fell in love with anyone he "saw" and liked to give them **bone-crushing "hugs."**
#0540

Future robots might be as small as **100 nanometers** (100 billionths of a meter) or 1,000 times smaller than the width of a human hair ...
#0541

... These tiny robots would be **small enough to explore the inside of a blood cell** and provide medical treatment.
#0542

The **iRobot Scooba** is built to scrub the smallest, dirtiest nooks and crannies, such as behind your toilet.
#0543

11 FREAKY FACTS ABOUT SPACE EXPLORATION

If you **farted** in a spacesuit, the **smell would stay inside.**

#0544

In 1961, Alan Shepard, the first American in space, realized that he needed to pee during his mission—but there was **no toilet!** So he peed **in his spacesuit!** #0545

Today, astronauts often wear **special diapers** during liftoff, reentry, and on space walks. #0546

Before going into space, astronauts have to train on a special zero-gravity toilet simulator. #0547

There are more than 500,000 pieces of **space junk** orbiting Earth. #0548

With little gravity in space, the liquids in your body move up toward your head, **filling your nose with snot.** #0549

If a **frog vomited in space,** the zero gravity would make it **throw up its stomach as well**. #0550

Some astronauts have reported that there is a **meaty-metallic smell** in space. While others report a **rum and raspberry smell**. #0551

Almost half of all astronauts suffer from **"space sickness,"** and zero-gravity vomit is hard to clean up! #0552

Space poop has to be sucked away, freeze-dried, and then stored to keep it from **floating around.** #0553

Sometimes, the bits of **freeze-dried poop** have floated free of the toilet, and astronauts have **caught them in their mouths** thinking they were **peanuts.** #0554

6 facts about Other Planets

Because of the **stronger gravity,** you would be **27 times heavier** on the Sun than on Earth (and a lot warmer). So if you weigh **220 lb** on Earth, you would weigh nearly **3 tons** on the surface of the Sun. #0555

Venus has 200-mph winds, a permanent toxic smog that traps heat close to the ground, and a surface **temperature of 840°F.** #0556

The rain on Venus is

sulfuric acid ...

... It would dissolve anything it touched— your spaceship, your umbrella, AND YOU.

#0557

Venus and Mars have atmospheres that are almost entirely made up of **CARBON DIOXIDE**. Breathing the air there would lead to **unconsciousness and then death**.

#0558

Jupiter, Saturn, Uranus, and Neptune are **giant balls of stinking gases** such as METHANE AND AMMONIA. Under the **thick layer of gas** is **liquid methane and ammonia**.

#0559

A storm on Mars can whip up a thick red

dust cloud

that can blanket the planet for **months.**

#0560

Before the storm   **After the storm**

127

5 REPELLENT PLANET

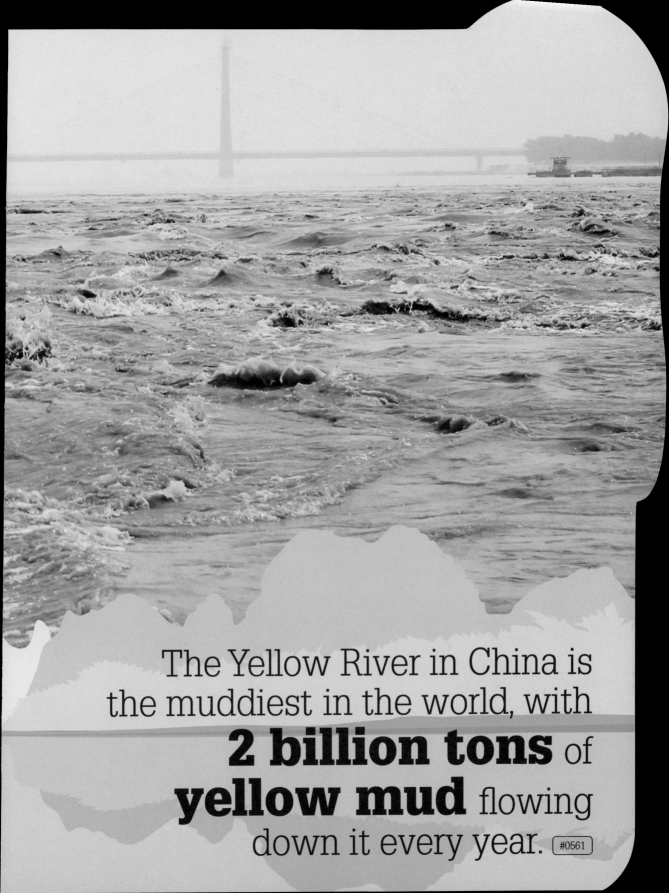

The Yellow River in China is the muddiest in the world, with **2 billion tons** of **yellow mud** flowing down it every year. #0561

11 facts about Rain forests

A mother **slow loris** licks her babies with her **poisonous saliva** to protect them from predators. #0562

Some **piranha fish** in the River Amazon attack in groups, **ripping the flesh off their prey.** #0563

Every second, an area of rain forest the size of a football field is cut down. #0565

The Amazon gets **9 ft of rain** every year— that's about the distance from your bedroom floor to the ceiling. #0566

Up until the early 20th century, rain forest **headhunters** killed intruders by **cutting off their heads.** They then boiled the heads, and **kept them as trophies.** #0564

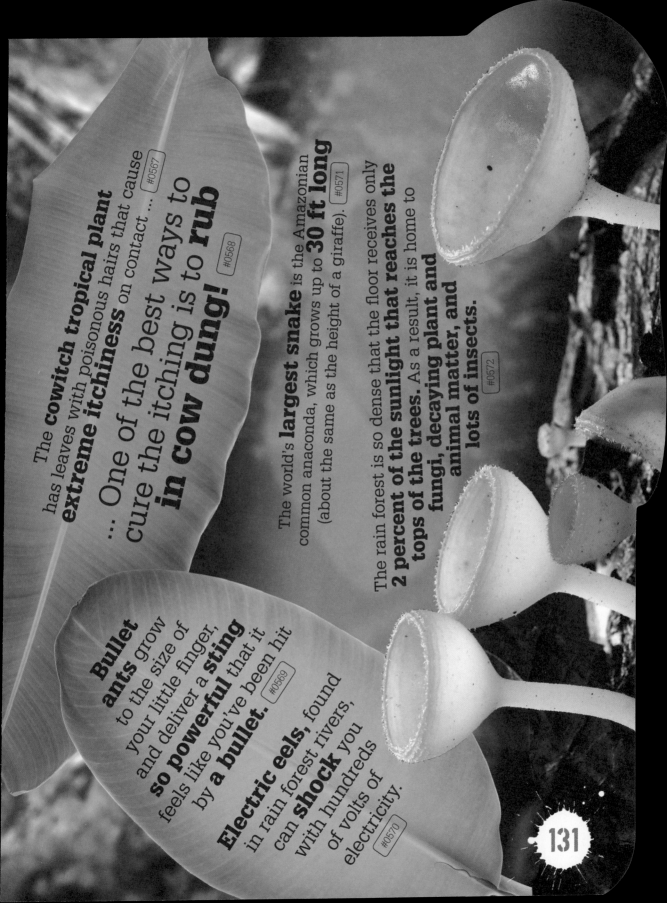

The **cowitch tropical plant** has leaves with poisonous hairs that cause **extreme itchiness** on contact... #0567

... One of the best ways to cure the itching is to **rub in cow dung!** #0568

The world's **largest snake** is the Amazonian common anaconda, which grows up to **30 ft long** (about the same as the height of a giraffe). #0571

The rain forest is so dense that the floor receives only **2 percent of the sunlight that reaches the tops of the trees.** As a result, it is home to **fungi, decaying plant and animal matter, and** lots of insects. #0572

Bullet ants grow to the size of your little finger, and deliver a **sting so powerful** that it feels like you've been hit **by a bullet.** #0569

Electric eels, found in rain forest rivers, can **shock** you with hundreds of volts of electricity. #0570

131

8 DEADLY DESERT FACTS

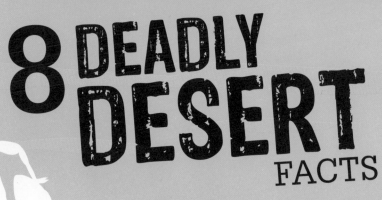

Deserts are places where **less than 10 in of rain** falls in a year. In July 1956, Unionville got **more than that in a single minute!**

#0573

The **deathstalker scorpion** likes to crawl into travelers' tents. A **bite** from this venomous critter can cause **months of pain,** and even **DEATH.** #0574

The **Gila monster,** a biting lizard, lives in the Mexican desert. It is **highly poisonous,** but it moves so slowly that it is not a great danger to humans.

#0575

A camel can shut its nose to keep out desert sand. #0576

A cactus plant's

dagger-sharp spines store water in the dry desert and also ensure that any hungry herbivore would think twice before munching on them. #0577

The kangaroo rat's **pee** comes out in the form of a **PASTE** so that it does not lose water. #0578

Desert-dwelling **dung beetles collect balls of poop,** which they roll around and store as food. #0579

Sheep's eyes are a delicacy in the north African desert. They are usually boiled up with the rest of the head, and offered as **TREATS**. #0580

133

8 CHILLY POLAR FACTS

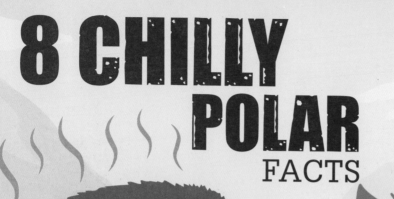

Male musk oxen are among the SMELLIEST CREATURES in the Arctic tundra. They release a **strong odor during mating season** to attract females, and they also like to mark their territory with **pee.**

#0531

In 1898, the ship **BELGICA** got stuck in the ice during an expedition to Antarctica. When the food ran out, the crew had to **eat penguins and seals.**

#0582

Scientists who visit Antarctica have to **take home all their trash, including pee and poop.**

#0583

Polar bears **HUNT SEALS,** biting into their heads to kill them.

#0584

In the freezing Arctic, extremities such as fingers and toes can suffer from **frostbite,** where the skin becomes **black** and **blistered.**

#0585

Frostbite can be treated by carefully re-heating the body. However, if the damage is too severe, the infected area may have to be **AMPUTATED.**

#0586

Polar explorers who don't wear protective goggles suffer from **snow blindness** when the strong UV light damages their eyes. It's a bit like having **sunburned eyes!**

#0587

The lion's mane jellyfish has **POISONOUS TENTACLES** that can trail up to **120 ft—** longer than a tennis court.

#0588

135

12 Grisly Mountain facts

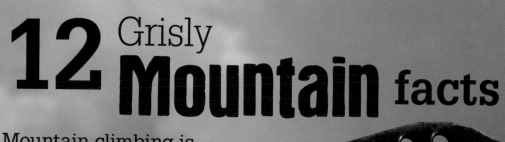

Mountain climbing is the **second most dangerous** sport in the world (the first is cave diving). #0589

When a passenger plane crashed in the Andes in 1972, the survivors stayed alive by **eating those who had died.** #0590

More than **40 bodies** have been found **frozen** on the climb up Mount Everest. #0591

Mount Everest is covered in trash, including discarded ropes and **piles of human poop** ... #0592

... In 2000, guides found over **600 discarded oxygen bottles** on Everest. #0593

High up, low air pressure causes body changes that lead to **altitude sickness,** which can make you tired, dizzy, and nauseous. #0594

Local guides around Everest think the best way to get rid of altitude sickness is eating **stinky garlic soup.** #0595

A 13,000-ft peak in the Swiss Alps called the **Eiger** is known as **"the murderous wall"** for its **dangerous climb.** #0596

In 1924, British mountaineer George Mallory disappeared on Everest. His body was found in 1999 at 27,000 ft. He hadn't made it to the top. #0599

K2 in the Himalayas is called the **"savage mountain."** One in four people who make it to the top **don't make it back down.** #0597

Some of the ice on Mont Blanc, France, is so **polluted by pee** that it has turned yellow. #0598

In 1995, **a 500-year-old frozen mummy** of a young girl was found near the top of Mount Ampato in southern Peru. #0600

11 facts about OCEANS

A **3,000-passenger** cruise liner generates about **8 tons of solid waste** per week. #0601

Swirling currents called **gyres** can appear in the ocean. These whirling currents can trap large amounts of **trash.** #0602

When waves break on parts of the shore, the water is pushed in **different directions** until it is forced back out toward the sea. The resulting **rip currents** can be **DEADLY.** #0603

In 2010, **five million barrels of oil were spilled** into the Gulf of Mexico, polluting thousands of square miles of water. #0604

In the South Pacific, there are more than **1,100 active volcanoes under water.** #0605

Dive deeper

than ½ mi into the ocean and you enter **the midnight zone**. It is pitch black, apart from a few **luminous animals.** #0606

Vents on the ocean floor pour out superheated chemicals and gases ... #0607

... **Bizarre life forms surround the vents**, including giant tubeworms, giant clams, and blind fish. #0608

Some underwater volcanoes **spew stinky methane and mud** instead of lava. #0609

Some little organisms feed entirely on the chemicals spewed out by underwater volcanoes. #0610

If you swallow ocean water, you'll also swallow **millions of viruses and bacteria.** #0611

11 foul facts about RIVERS

About **265,000,000 gallons of raw sewage** is dumped into the Ganges River in India and Bangladesh every day. #0613

40 percent of the U.S.'s rivers are too polluted for fishing, swimming, or to sustain aquatic life. #0612

> **However, many of the 420 million people** who live near the Ganges rely on the water for washing and drinking. #0614

Bacteria levels in the Ganges are
3,000 times
above the level that is considered safe. #0615

More than half of the world's
500 major rivers are badly polluted. #0616

Found in the River Amazon, anacondas eat fish, birds, mammals, and other reptiles. Sometimes, **hungry females even eat males.** #0617

If you **pee** in the River Nile, Egypt, **parasitic worms could find their way into your body** by following the warm pee trail. #0618

Up to a third of male fish in U.K. rivers are in the process of changing sex due to pollution, specifically the female hormones found in human sewage. #0619

In 1858, the smell of raw sewage from the River Thames in the U.K. was so bad that Parliament was dissolved. **It was known as the "GREAT STINK."** #0620

The River Congo in West Central Africa is the **world's most dangerous river.** Rapids surge through a **75-mi impassable canyon** known as the **Gates of Hell.** #0621

The aggressive **BULL SHARK** swims up freshwater rivers and **attacks prey** in shallow water. #0622

141

10 Wicked Weather facts

The 1815 eruption of **Mount Tambora,** Indonesia, threw out so much dust that the sun was blotted out. Temperatures around the world fell, and there was no summer in Europe that year.
#0623

If a cloud is so low to the ground that it's impossible to tell where snow-covered land ends and the cloud begins, you are in a **whiteout.** #0624

Russians joke that their greatest weapon is **"General Winter."** The severe Russian winter has frozen the guns and troops of several invading armies. #0625

Each year, there are about **10,000 big thunderstorms** and **1,000 tornadoes and hurricanes** in the U.S. #0626

In 1955, a girl riding a horse in South Dakota, was **sucked inside a tornado**. Both the horse and the girl landed safely after traveling **nearly a mile** in the air. #0627

The deadliest single tornado was the "Tri-state" tornado that **killed 695 people** in Missouri, Illinois, and Indiana in March 1925. #0628

Falling air pressure can create a violent wind known as a "bomb." In 1987, a "bomb" flattened **15 million trees** in England. #0629

The temperature of a lightning bolt can reach **54,000°F.** #0630

Lightning strikes somewhere on Earth about **100 times every second.** #0631

In the U.S., about **50 people** a year are **struck dead** by a bolt of lightning. #0632

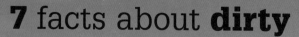

7 facts about dirty
Beaches

Shellfish such as mussels filter out **raw sewage** from water and eat it. #0633

The smell of the seaside is caused by **slimy rotting seaweed** trapped under sand or rocks. #0634

In 2007, volunteers picked up **3,000 tons of trash** across 76 countries—that is as heavy as **600 elephants.** #0635

In 2008, an unknown beast called the **"Montauk monster"** was washed up on a New York beach. Scientists still haven't been able to identify it. #0636

In 2011, **6,000 dead ducks and gulls** washed up on a Canadian beach after eating contaminated fish. #0637

In 2012, a **fish eye the size of a tennis ball** was found on a beach in Florida. No one is sure what species it came from. #0638

The white sand on coral beaches contains lots of **parrotfish poop.** #0639

145

9 facts about hot and cold

At **-47°F,** human flesh freezes in about 1 minute.

#0640

When you get REALLY COLD, **your blood pressure rises** as blood vessels constrict to reduce heat loss. In response, your kidneys get rid of fluid to lower your blood pressure again, making you want to pee more.

#0641

If you don't wear **goggles** in **high-wind-chill conditions,** the **corneas** of your eyes can freeze.

#0642

Miliaria

or "prickly heat" can happen when you **sweat too much** in hot weather, causing an **itchy, stinging rash.**

#0644

Heat edema is the pooling of fluids under the skin in **extreme heat,** causing **hands or legs** to SWELL UP.

#0643

On July 10th, 1913, temperatures in **Death Valley, California,** were recorded at **135°F** in the shade—**the hottest ever.** #0645

Sunburn actually **DAMAGES YOUR D.N.A.,** destroying skin cells, which is why you peel after a really bad burn.

#0646

Drinking too much water can cause low sodium in the blood, resulting in **vomiting, headaches, fatigue, cramps, or even a coma.** It is known as **HYPONATREMIA.**

#0647

Extreme heat makes you **sweat lots,** which can lead to **dehydration.** This is known as **HYPERNATREMIA.**

#0648

12 soggy facts about

Rain AND hail

Tornadoes and water spouts can pick up **SMALL ANIMALS.** Later, they rain back down to earth as frozen animal lumps. #0649

In 1863, a farmer in Quebec, Canada, found a **frog** inside a large hailstone. #0650

In 1873, **a storm of frogs** fell on the state of Missouri. #0652

In 2001, some mysterious red rain fell on Kerala, India. It took its color from airborne fungal spores. #0651

The people of Tasmania, Australia, found a **SLIMY JELLIED RAIN** on their properties the morning after a big thunderstorm. It is believed to have been fish eggs or jellyfish. #0653

Fungal spores in soil release an **odor** that gives rainwater its distinctive smell. #0654

On July 14th, 1953, **golf-ball-sized hailstones** fell in Alberta, Canada, **killing 36,000 ducks.** #0655

In 1890, **blood rained from the sky** in Calabria, Italy. The blood was thought to have come from birds killed by violent winds. #0656

The **biggest hailstone** ever recorded was more than 8 in wide— that's **bigger than a softball.** #0658

A **shower of herring fish** fell on the town of Bournemouth, U.K., in 1948. #0657

In 1976, a **gigantic flash flood** swept down the Big Thompson River Canyon in Colorado, after three quarters of the area's annual rainfall fell in **just 4 hours.** #0660

Some people are **allergic to rain,** and touching it causes swelling and redness. #0659

149

10 FREEZING FACTS ABOUT SNOW

Thundersnow **is a BLIZZARD** that happens in a thunderstorm. Often **snow will fall** and **lightning will strike** at the same time. #0661

A really bad **snowstorm** can dump more than **40 million tons** of snow over a large city. #0662

New York had 2 ft of snow during the winter of 2011. **Rat-infested sofas and rotten garbage were found on the streets** after it melted. #0663

From **1998** to **1999, 100 ft** of snow fell on Mount Baker— enough to bury a ten-story building. #0664

An **ARIZONA** snow resort filled its slopes with fake snow made entirely out of urine.
#0665

Snow gathers lots of **POLLUTION** and dirt from the air as it falls.
#0666

Some algae can grow in settled snow,
#0667

making the snow change color.

If you eat **snow** when you're stuck in a **blizzard,** it will make you **colder** and even more dehydrated.
#0668

Dutchman Wim Hof **ran a half marathon barefoot** in the snow in 2 hours 16 minutes.
#0669

Some **SNOW ALGAE** is also known as WATERMELON SNOW, because it smells fruity and has a red tinge. However, eating it will make you **sick.**
#0670

151

9 facts about **CLIMATE CHANGE**

Ocean water is becoming **MORE ACIDIC** because of **increased carbon dioxide emissions.** This causes growth disorders in some marine animals.
#0671

Warm oceans cause coral to bleach, and eventually die. #0672

Past climate conditions can be worked out by **studying the remains of dead beetles**—different beetles lived in different climates. #0673

After the last Ice Age, seawater expanded and ice melted, causing **sea levels to rise by 425 ft**—that's the height of a 40-story building. #0674

Global warming is **causing water levels to rise.** Small island nations, such as Tuvalu in the Pacific, are in danger of disappearing altogether.
#0675

As the northern hemisphere gets warmer,

DISEASE-CARRYING PESTS

such as mosquitoes
will move north. #0676

Scientists list
12 diseases called the

DEADLY DOZEN

that will spread because of
climate change. These include
yellow fever, cholera, and
bubonic plague.

#0677

The rise in
temperatures due
to global warming
will make people more
susceptible to heat
rashes and other skin
complaints.

#0678

Methane

is a greenhouse gas,
which traps radiated
heat in the atmosphere,
warming up the Earth. It
can be generated by **cow
dung** and **cow farts**.

#0679

153

12 DISGUSTING DINOSAUR FACTS

Scientists have learned much about prehistoric life by studying **COPROLITES—fossilized dinosaur droppings.** #0680

Sometimes, dinosaurs would become trapped in **pits of goopy tar and mud. The skeletons of these trapped animals** would then be preserved as **fossils.**

#0681

The **MILLIONS OF TONS OF POOP** made by dinosaurs every day made the ground fertile. #0682

Little bits of bone have been found in **TYRANNOSAURUS COPROLITES,** showing how they could crunch up the bones of their prey.

#0684

A huge **coprolite** made by a dinosaur called a Maiasaura, was found in Wyoming. It was the **size** and **shape** of a **basketball.** #0683

The **preserved stomach contents** of dinosaurs have been found in some fossils. **The remains show diets ranging from seeds and plants to whole animals.** #0685

Sauropod dinosaurs would **swallow big stones** called **gastroliths** to help them digest food. #0686

A Tyrannosaurus rex could eat up to **50 LB OF MEAT** in one bite, which is the equivalent of more than **100 steaks.** #0687

The world's oldest **FOSSILIZED VOMIT** was discovered in 2002. It was made by an ichthyosaur, a marine reptile that lived at the same time as the dinosaurs. #0689

The meat-eating theropod dinosaurs had **SERRATED, KNIFELIKE TEETH** to help them rip apart flesh. #0688

The **Irritator** was a big meat-eating spinosaur, so-named because a frustrated scientist had to spend hours piecing together its broken skull. #0690

Velociraptors had one long, **curved claw** on each of their hind legs, which they would use to slash at prey to make them bleed to death. #0691

155

11 facts about LIFE IN THE PAST

Trilobites were ancient bugs related to insects and spiders. They had a **HARD skeleton** on the outside of their bodies that they replaced in order to grow. #0692

Underneath a trilobite's skeleton was a **squishy** body, with several parts moving freely to help them wriggle about. #0693

350 million years ago, the high levels of oxygen in the atmosphere allowed insects to grow larger than rats. #0694

Arthropleura was a MONSTROUS MILLIPEDE that grew **10 ft long**—longer than the diamondback rattlesnake. #0695

Many species have died out in the **"mass extinction events"** that have occurred through history, in which MOST LIFE ON EARTH WAS WIPED OUT.

#0696

Dunkleosteus was a fish that **lived in the ocean 380–360 million years ago.** It was over **30 ft long,** and had a ferocious bite.

#0697

The **giant dragonfly** meganeura had a wingspan of 2½ ft— that's BIGGER THAN A PIGEON.

#0698

There have been several **VERY COLD PERIODS IN THE PAST 2 million** years, during which species died out, and new ones emerged.

#0699

Some mass extinction events were very sudden, such as the meteorite impact that wiped out the dinosaurs

65 million years ago ...

#0701

More than **650 MILLION YEARS AGO,** Earth froze over completely, and looked like a giant snowball.

#0700

... The explosion threw up so much **ash** that the sun was hidden, temperatures fell, and no large animal was **able to survive.**

#0702

6 GROSS

New York City is home to **8 million people** and ......

PEOPLE

250,000 rats—
that's 1 rat for every 36 people. #0703

13 GRIMY FACTS ABOUT CITIES

Manila, the capital of the Philippines, is so crowded that there are **104,995 people** crammed into each square mile, roughly **4 times** the density of New York City. #0704

In December 2005, air pollution was so bad in **Tehran, Iran,** that

1,600 people were hospitalized. #0705

Air pollution is a huge problem in **Mexico City** because it is in a valley. A **blanket of smog** caused by cars and factories is often visible over the city. #0706

Urban foxes eat almost anything—**slugs, worms, rats ...** #0707

Traffic jams in São Paulo, Brazil, are so bad that many people spend **five hours a day** driving to and from work. #0708

... But a fox's favorite meal is whatever it can find in the nearest trash can! #0709

London, U.K., has more **urban foxes** than it does **buses.** #0710

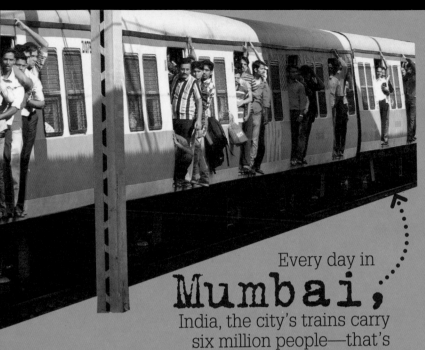

Every day in
Mumbai,
India, the city's trains carry six million people—that's the same as the whole population of Israel. #0712

San Pedro Sula in Honduras
is so dangerous that in 2011, **1,143 people** were murdered. That's more than **3 MURDERS** per day.

#0713

At least **30 percent** of the drinking water in **Singapore** comes from **recycled water,** including some from **toilets.**

#0714

Ulaanbaatar
in Mongolia is the **world's coldest capital city.**
The temperature remains below freezing from November to March, and an 8-in-thick layer of snow covers the city. #0715

PYONGYANG, NORTH KOREA,
has so many power cuts that many people avoid the metro train in case they get trapped underground.

#0716

9 facts about GARBAGE

Mumbai, India, gets rid of the horrid smell of its garbage dump by pouring **hundreds of gallons of deodorant on it.**

#0717

The **Citarum River** in Indonesia is filled with the garbage of **9 million people,** plus the liquid waste of **500 factories ...**

#0718

... In places, the water can no longer be seen beneath the moving carpet of garbage ...

#0719

... Boatmen still go on the river, but not to fish. **They look for things in the garbage to sell.**

#0720

The Pacific is home to the **Great Pacific Garbage Patch,** a vast soup of debris and chemical sludge that covers nearly **2,000 mi².**
#0721

About **14 billion lb of garbage** is dumped into the oceans every year, **most of it plastic.**
#0722

When garbage decomposes in a landfill, it produces methane gas—that's the smelly gas **in farts.** #0723

In a landfill, cigarette butts take 12 years to biodegrade. **"Disposable" diapers take 800 years** to biodegrade. #0724

Until the early 20th century, thrown-out food was mixed with **animal remains** to make a greasy gunk used in soaps and candles. #0725

163

9 facts about POLLUTION

Linfen, China, is one of the most **polluted cities** on the planet due to the coal dust produced by the city's mines ...

#0726

In Ranipet, India, the **water in local rivers is SO TOXIC** that it **feels like an insect bite** when it touches the skin.

#0727

... In fact, 16 of the world's 20 most polluted cities are in **China.**

#0728

Over **1 BILLION people in the world** do not have access to **clean drinking water** and **5,000 people die** each day due to **dirty drinking water.**

#0729

Some oceans have **dead zones—**

nothing can live there

because pollution has caused an

oxygen shortage. #0730

If you see
COTTON SWABS
on a beach,
DON'T SWIM THERE.
People flush them down
the loo, so they're a sign
that **untreated poop
has flowed into
the water.** #0731

LONDON, U.K., was once so
THICKLY POLLUTED with coal smoke
that it created a thick fog known
as a **"pea souper."** #0732

**Swimming and fishing
are banned** in Onondago Lake,
New York State, because it has so much
sewage and industrial waste. #0733

.........>

The **ACROPOLIS**
is a collection of
ruined buildings in
Athens, Greece.
Acid rain has caused
these old buildings
to **crumble** more **in
the last 40 years**
than they did in the
previous 2,500. #0734

11 facts about yucky FESTIVALS

In the Rattlesnake roundup in Sweetwater, Texas, **contestants take part in a rattlesnake-eating contest.** #0735

At Thorrablot, a midwinter feast in Iceland, **seal flippers** and **rotting shark** meat are served. #0736

In the **Blobfest** of Pennsylvania, the crowd reenact scenes from the old horror movie, *The Blob.* #0737

During the Interstate Mullet Toss, **mullet fish are thrown over the state line** between Alabama and Florida. #0738

THE WORLD BOG SNORKELING CHAMPIONSHIP, held in Wales, U.K., has contestants snorkeling through deep puddles of sludge. #0740

Every year in July, people try to **outrun a group of bulls** through the **streets of Pamplona,** Spain, to prove their bravery. Up to **300 PEOPLE** are injured every time. #0739

In the town of Ivrea, Italy, rival teams **throw oranges at each other** during the BATTLE OF THE ORANGES, which is held every February. #0741

Every year in Thailand, people present fruit and vegetables to the local monkey population at the **Monkey** Buffet Festival. #0742

In spring, **Hindus throw colored paint at each other** during the festival of **Holi.** #0743

In Mali, there's a **mud-plastering festival** each spring, when everyone **slaps mud** on the buildings and themselves. #0744

In August, **Spaniards do battle** in the world's biggest **tomato fight,** known as **La Tomatina**, on the streets of **Buñol, Valencia.** #0745

167

8 grim facts about BUILDINGS

Poop mixed with **straw** is used to make bricks in some countries. #0746

The ancient Egyptian pyramids were actually **tombs,** built to hold the **mummified bodies** of the pharaohs (kings). #0747

In tropical countries, the tiny **pharaoh ant** is a major pest in hospitals and offices. They breed huge colonies in **between sheets of paper!** #0748

The stones in an African rondavel (a type of house) are stuck together **USING COW POOP.** #0749

Wembley Stadium in the U.K. has **2,618 toilets,** more than any other venue in the world. #0750

Poor airflow, mold and toxic paint can cause **"Sick Building Syndrome" (SBS).** #0751

SBS has a variety of symptoms including **headaches, nausea, throat irritation, a runny nose, and skin rashes.** #0752

In New York, a kids' playground was built out of pure steel. **The steel heated to**

10 stinky facts about FARMING

Before the invention of chemical fertilizers, farmers' fields were fertilized with **animal dung** and **human poop.** #0754

A third of all the fruit and vegetables we eat contain chemical pesticides

SPRAYED ON THE FIELDS

where they were grown.

#0755

There are more than **50 BILLION** chickens in the world— outnumbering people by more than 7 to 1. #0756

Each day, the world's chickens produce

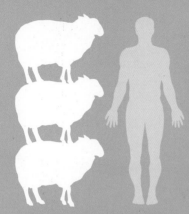

In Wales, U.K., there are
THREE TIMES
more sheep than people.

#0758

HAGGIS
is a traditional dish in Scotland, U.K. It is made of minced sheep **heart, liver,** and **lungs,** and wrapped in the lining of the sheep's **stomach.**

#0760

MUTTON BUSTING is a popular sport in some rodeo shows—children ride **sheep** instead of **bulls.**

#0759

Dairy cows provide
90%
of the world's milk supply.
The best cows provide nearly 7 gal of milk per day—that's **100** glasses of milk!

#0761

A cow could walk up some stairs, but would have trouble walking down again—its knees don't **BEND THE RIGHT WAY.**

#0762

There are around **1 billion pigs** in the world, and half of them live in CHINA.

#0763

11 facts about SEWERS

In Victorian London, **HUMAN SEWAGE** drained into the River Thames, turning the **drinking water brown.**
#0764

In Mexico City in 2000, heavy rain broke down the wall of a sewage canal. **Thousands of homes were flooded 3 ft high with sewage.**
#0765

In 1848, a law was passed in the U.K. stating that all houses should have an **ash pit, where poop and pee fell into a pile of ash** ready for collection.
#0766

London built a modern sewer system after the **"GREAT STINK" OF 1858 WHEN A SMELL OF POOP** hung over the city.
#0767

Toilet paper was first used in **China** more than **1,500 years ago.**
#0768

Before toilet paper was widely available, rich people used **wool, lace,** or **hemp** to wipe their bottoms, while the poor used **rags, leaves, sand, or their hands.**

#0769

The average person will go to the toilet about **2,500** times a year and spend **3 years** on the toilet in their lifetime!

#0770

The toilet nearest the entrance in a public bathroom is **likely to be the cleanest** because it is used least often.

#0771

If you use a composting toilet, microorganisms **break down the sewage into compost.**

#0772

In New South Wales, Australia, so many **frogs invaded the public bathrooms** that the toilets stopped working.

#0773

Rats are good underwater swimmers and can swim up pipes and **INTO YOUR TOILET.**

#0774

173

11 rotten facts about LIFE ON SHIP

Ship's biscuits, known as **HARDTACK,** were eaten by sailors from the 16th century. They were baked up to **6 months** in advance of a voyage and could last for many years …

#0775

… The biscuits were so **HARD** that they were said to be able to stop a **bullet.**

#0776

The maiden voyage of the **TITANIC** was very **smelly.** More than 700 third-class passengers had **two bathtubs** between them.

#0777

Weevils and maggots were fond of hardtack so sailors tapped their biscuits to get rid of any **creepy crawlies.**

#0778

Sailors who fell asleep on duty or **did a poop** onboard instead of overboard could be **disciplined.**

#0779

174

The most severe discipline was to be lashed by the **CAT-O'-NINE-TAILS**—a multi-tailed whip. #0780

After the punishment, the wounds were washed with **seawater** to prevent infection, but this caused **EXTRA PAIN.** #0781

In the early 19th century, convicts were shipped to **Australia.** Conditions were so terrible that many died on the journey, which took up to **six months.** #0782

Convicts were kept below deck in chains most of the time and got very seasick. The galleys were

AWASH WITH VOMIT.
#0783

By the time they arrived, many had **TYPHOID AND CHOLERA,** or were weakened by **SCURVY, DYSENTERY, OR FEVER.** #0784

Today, about **60** large ships sink or run aground every day. #0785

13 FREAKY FLYING FACTS

In the 16th century, Italian **Paolo Guidotti made wings from whalebone and feathers** and attempted to fly. He fell through the roof of a church and broke his leg. #0786

In 1928, wealthy businessman Alfred Lowenstein mistook the door of his airplane for the toilet and plunged **4,000 ft** into the English Channel. #0787

Midair panic was caused by a Sri Lankan cricketer in 2013 when he tried **to open the door** of an airplane thinking it was the toilet. #0788

Pre packed airline food often tastes bland. That's because the aircraft's **noise distracts your senses** from noticing taste. #0789

Airline tea tastes funny because the cabin pressure means the **water boils at 194°F instead of 212°F—** not hot enough to make a decent brew. #0790

In January 2009, a U.S. passenger flight had to make an emergency landing on the Hudson River when a **flock of geese flew into both engines** ... #0791

... All 155 passengers and crew survived,

BUT THE GEESE DID NOT. #0792

Niek Vermeulen from the Netherlands has the world's largest collection of airline sickness bags ... #0793

... He's collected 6,016 **"BARF BAGS"** from **1,142** different airlines.
#0794

Toilet waste is stored in a huge **TANK** inside the plane and sucked out at the end of a flight.
#0795

In 2004, Virgin Atlantic introduced **Design for Chunks,** a competition to design sickness bags. #0796

In 2013, a British woman found a frozen block of airline poop and pee that had crashed into her house. #0797

In 2013, passengers on a 13-hour flight suffered from a **violent vomiting** and **diarrhea bug**—and there were only four toilets on the plane. #0798

7 foul facts about Railroads

The earliest passenger trains in the U.K. had three classes of travel—first and second class were comfortable carriages, but third-class passengers had to ride in **open-top** goods wagons, seated on **wooden benches.** #0799

U.S. steam locomotives were fitted with a V-shaped device at the front. They were known as **cowcatchers** and were designed to push away obstacles on the track, such as cows. #0800

Indian Railways carry more than **25 million passengers** every day, which is the same as the populations of Norway and Greece combined. #0801

People often leave strange things on trains. In 2009, **a dead octopus** was handed into Edinburgh Waverley station in the U.K. #0802

In 2011, four bags of **VENOMOUS COBRAS** were left on a passenger train in Vietnam. #0803

Waste from train toilets is usually **flushed straight onto the tracks.** #0804

16 percent of Dutch trains **do not have toilets** so in 2011 Dutch National Railways introduced **"PEE BAGS."** In a toilet emergency, commuters can request one of the special plastic bags from the train conductor. #0805

179

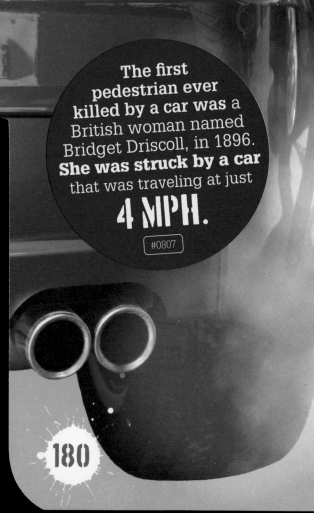

11 CHOKING FACTS ABOUT CARS

16% of car owners never wash their cars.

#0806

The first pedestrian ever killed by a car was a British woman named Bridget Driscoll, in 1896. **She was struck by a car** that was traveling at just **4 MPH.**

#0807

Driving motor vehicles releases more **AIR POLLUTION** than any other **human activity.**

#0808

"DIRTIER" cars emit their own weight in carbon gases **every six weeks.**

#0809

In 2009, spindle ermine caterpillars span a silk COCOON around a car to protect themselves while they **transformed into butterflies.** #0810

Alternative car fuels being tested include **sawdust, nuts, used diapers, chocolate, cow poop,** and **turkey guts.** #0811

In 2008, a U.S. plastic surgeon claimed to have turned fat drained from his patients into biofuel. #0812

Some people are experimenting with waste vegetable oil **(W.V.O)** or chip fat as a cleaner fuel for cars! #0813

In 2010, the Bio-Bug car made its debut. It runs on biogas produced by

HUMAN WASTE!

#0814

The kea, an alpine parrot native to New Zealand, **likes to nibble on cars.** #0815

In 2005, a British company launched the Indipod, an **in-car toilet.** #0816

8 scary facts about Schools

In Victorian England, teachers often punished pupils by **beating them with a cane ...** #0817

... Boys were usually caned on their **backsides** ... #0818

... Girls were either beaten on their **bare legs** or across their **hands.** #0819

"Punishment baskets" were used in some Victorian classrooms to suspend **badly behaved children** from the ceiling. #0820

Pupils who were slow learners had to wear a pointy **"dunce's cap"** or donkey's ears. #0821

School food is famously bad—one of the worst dishes was **"turkey twizzlers,"** which contained **only 34 percent** turkey. The rest was mostly grain. #0822

Many kids become **anxious, frightened,** or **nauseous** about going to school. This is called

didaskaleinophobia or scolionophobia.
#0823

In ancient Sparta, 7-year-old boys at military school slept on beds of **sharp reeds** to get them used to pain. #0824

5 facts about PRISONS

In some old prisons, there is no toilet in a cell, so inmates have to use a bucket. Every morning, they have to **"SLOP OUT"** and carry their own waste to the drains.

#0825

Rikers Island Prison in New York is the **world's largest** prison, occupying 395 acres—the equivalent in size to

320

White Houses.

#0826

The U.S. has the world's **biggest** prisoner population— **716 prisoners per 100,000 people.**

#0827

The **smallest** prisoner population is in the city state of San Marino, Italy, which had only **one prisoner** in 2011.

#0828

Victorian prisoners ate a VERY BORING DIET—they usually ate porridge for breakfast, soup for lunch, and porridge for dinner.

#0829

11 GROSS FACTS ABOUT HOMES

Every time you flush the toilet, **you send an invisible 6-ft plume of bacteria** into the air that lands on exposed surfaces.

#0830

The toilet is not the dirtiest place in the bathroom,

IT'S THE SINK.

The sink has **130,000 germs** per square inch, but the toilet seat only has **130 germs per square inch.**

#0831

Locals in Florida found that **Cuban tree frogs** had swum up their pipes into their toilet bowls.

#0832

A kitchen chopping board has **200 percent** more bacteria than the average **toilet seat.** #0833

Mice can squeeze through **cracks as small as ¼ in** to get into your house, and nest under the floor. #0834

Brown rat droppings are like mouse poop, but **three times larger.** #0835

Mouse droppings are easy to identify because they are **¼ in long, black** and **shaped like grains of rice.** #0836

Black rat droppings are more **sausage-shaped,** and look like fatter jelly beans. #0837

Bat droppings look like mouse droppings but are **shiny, speckled,** and **always found in a pile.** #0838

COCKROACH POOP looks like small dark specks. #0839

#0840

Bird poop contains **acid,** which eats into house bricks and damages them.

187

7 YUCKY

FOOD

Garum was the ancient Romans' and Greeks' favorite sauce ...

#0841

... It was made from **ROTTEN FISH.**

#0842

14 FACTS ABOUT EATING INSECTS

More than
1,900 SPECIES OF INSECT
are eaten around the world. #0843

Fried locusts are a Nigerian delicacy. They taste a bit like prawns. #0844

Japanese athletes drink

GIANT
HORNET JUICE.
This is a sports drink made from the stomach juices of **giant hornet larvae.** #0845

In Cambodia, **large spiders fried with garlic are a popular dish.** #0846

American Indians
ROAST BEETLES
and eat them like popcorn. #0848

People in Bali, Indonesia, catch **dragonflies** with a stick coated in sticky plant juice, grill them, and then eat them. #0847

Food markets in Beijing, China, offer **candied scorpions on a stick.** #0849

Japanese restaurants may offer boiled **wasp larvae** or fried **SILK MOTH PUPAE.** #0850

Thousands of Bogong moths return to the **Bogong mountains** of Australia to breed every year, where people gather them up and eat them. #0851

The **witchetty grub** is a white moth **larva** the size of a **large finger**—it is a favorite food of Aboriginal Australians. #0852

In Mexico, **chapulines** are **grasshoppers** that are toasted with **CHILI** or garlic. #0853

In Laos, people eat **red ants** with egg tossed in a salad. #0854

In 2012, Dutch university professor Marcel Dicke published **The Insect Cookbook.**

He wanted to show people that insects can be a tasty source of protein. #0855

In 2013, a group of London art students **opened a restaurant** specializing in insects. Dishes included **watermelon** with **caterpillar risotto** and **ground-up cricket.** #0856

12 FOOD-EATING RECORD facts

Roman Emperor Nero started eating **dinner** in the **afternoon** and finished around **dawn.** The food included jellyfish, boiled tree fungi, and flamingo. #0857

In 2006, Japanese eating champion Takeru Kobayashi ate **97 HAMBURGERS** in **10 minutes,** beating his own world record by 28. #0858

Every day, Americans consume about 20 million hamburgers and 9 million pizzas. #0859

American Joe Chestnut is a world champion competitive eater. **In 2013, he beat his own record by scoffing**

69 HOT DOGS IN 10 MINUTES. #0860

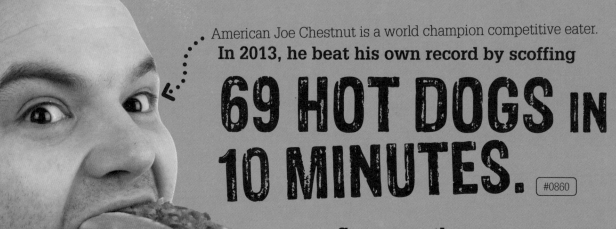

Sumo wrestlers eat two giant pots of meat stew every day to make sure they're heavy enough to fight. #0861

For breakfast, Olympic swimmer Michael Phelps ate **three fried-egg sandwiches, a five-egg omelet, toast topped with sugar, and three pancakes.** For lunch, he ate **a huge bowl of pasta.** #0862

American Tim Janus can put away **140 PIECES OF SUSHI, in 6 minutes.** #0863

The largest number of **oysters swallowed in 3 minutes is 233.** #0864

Korean-American Sonya Thomas holds 20 food-eating records. One record involved eating **44 LOBSTERS** in 12 minutes. #0867

Gary Bashaw Junior once mixed milk and chocolate powder in his mouth, then squirted 2 oz of milkshake out of his nose. #0865

Over a **BILLION PEOPLE** around the world **are overweight,** which is about the same number as those who are made **ill from hunger.** #0866

American Don Lerman ate **seven 4 oz sticks of salted butter** in 5 minutes. #0868

193

12 FACTS ABOUT INDIGESTION

Symptoms of indigestion include an **ache** in your stomach, **vomiting, bloating,** and **heartburn.** #0869

Indigestion usually happens when you **eat too much food,** eat too fast, or eat something that disagrees with you. #0870

Spicy foods seasoned with **chili** and **peppers** can also give you indigestion. #0871

Heartburn happens when **stomach acid** splashes back up into the gullet (the tube running from your mouth to your stomach). #0872

Doctors look inside your stomach during an **endoscopy,** when they put a camera **down your throat.** #0873

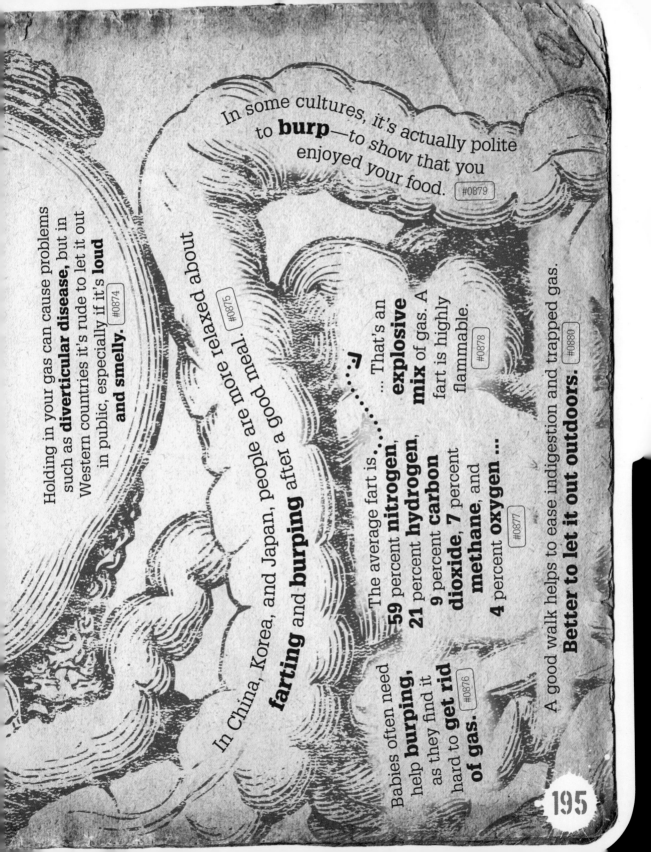

In some cultures, it's actually polite to **burp**—to show that you enjoyed your food. #0879

Holding in your gas can cause problems such as **diverticular disease,** but in Western countries it's rude to let it out in public, especially if it's **loud and smelly.** #0874

In China, Korea, and Japan, people are more relaxed about **farting** and **burping** after a good meal. #0875

Babies often need help **burping,** as they find it hard to **get rid of gas.** #0876

The average fart is… … That's an **explosive mix** of gas. A fart is highly flammable. #0878

The average fart is **59 percent nitrogen, 21 percent hydrogen, 9 percent carbon dioxide, 7 percent methane,** and **4 percent oxygen** … #0877

A good walk helps to ease indigestion and trapped gas. **Better to let it out outdoors.** #0880

195

9 VITAL VITAMIN Facts

You can get scurvy if you don't eat enough food with vitamin C. Symptoms include **INTERNAL BLEEDING, TEETH FALLING OUT, SWOLLEN GUMS, MADNESS, and even death ...**

#0881

Sailors on long voyages were prone to **scurvy** and wrongly believed they could avoid it by eating mustard or drinking vinegar.

#0882

In 1520, Portuguese explorer Vasco da Gama **lost 208 of his crew of 220 to scurvy.**

#0883

... Your legs will also get very **swollen** and you'll **have to keep going** to the **TOILET.**

#0884

Scurvy is not common today, but in 2012, a student in the U.S. contracted the disease. His diet had included **packets of sugar for breakfast and poptarts for lunch.** #0885

196

About one third of children under five suffer from **VITAMIN A** deficiency. In extreme cases, it can cause **blindness** or **death.** #0886

Not getting enough sunlight can affect your body's ability to process **VITAMIN D.** A lack of vitamin D can cause **RICKETS,** a disease in which **bones and muscles become soft and deformed.** #0887

A LACK OF **VITAMIN B7** can cause **hair loss, anemia, tiredness, hallucinations,** and **depression.** #0888

Not eating enough **VITAMIN B12** can cause **HYPOCOBALAMINEMIA.** Symptoms include **anemia, swollen stomach, and brain and nervous system malfunctions.** #0889

11 YUCKY FACTS ABOUT
FOOD FROM HISTORY

DRINKS

In ancient Egypt, everyone, including children, drank barley beer. It was more like a cloudy, **lumpy soup** than modern beer. #0890

Some ancient Chinese dynasties liked to gulp down **whole snakes** soaked in wine. #0891

DELICACIES

Roman Emperor Nero treated his guests to several tasty delicacies including **dormice** sprinkled with poppyseed, **cow's udders,** and a **hare** with "wings" attached to it. #0892

The Aztecs invented chocolate, but they did not add sugar and drank it as a liquid, rather than eating it in its solid form. #0893

MAINS

The Manchu Han Imperial Feast, a **108-course** banquet in ancient China, included dishes such as **camel's hump**, **bear's paws**, **monkey's brains**, **rhinoceros tails**, and **deer tendons.** #0894

It was once common to eat **seagulls**, either baked or in pies. #0895

Medieval plague cures included eating powdered stag's horn, powdered pearls, and emeralds—none of which worked. #0896

Henry I of England got ill and eventually died after eating too many lamprey fish. #0897

In 1455, the Count of Anjou, France, served a feast of enormous pies, each containing **a whole deer**, **a duck**, **6 chickens**, **10 pigeons**, **a rabbit**, and **26 boiled eggs**. #0898

DESSERT

In 1817, the Prince Regent of England held a banquet at which a 4-ft Turkish mosque made entirely of **marzipan** was served. #0899

In parts of the U.S., it was once quite common to eat **bear pie.** #0900

13 CANNIBAL
FACTS

One of the Aztecs' favorite recipes was a **human stew** called **"tlacatlaolli."** #0901

In the Middle Ages, some people ground up **ancient Egyptian mummies** to make medicine. #0902

Aztec priests ritually sacrificed enemies, **ripping their hearts out** and **eating their bodies.** #0904

Hot human blood, distilled brains, and **powdered human heart** have all been used as possible cures for epilepsy. #0903

The Korowai tribe on southeast Papua were cannibals **up until the 1970s,** when they met outsiders for the first time. #0905

"Mellified man" medicine, made from **soaking a human corpse in honey,** was used in Arabia in the 1100s. #0906

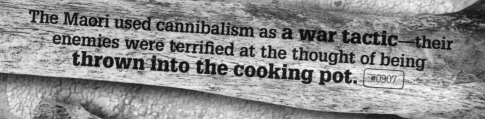

The Maori used cannibalism as **a war tactic**—their enemies were terrified at the thought of being **thrown into the cooking pot.** #0907

In the early 20th century, chief Ratu Udre Udre of Fiji is said to have eaten **872 people.** #0908

"Long pig" is a cannibal code word for cooked human. #0909

Biting your fingernails is technically **self-cannibalism ...** #0910

... As is eating your own hair, which can make **hairballs** in your stomach ... #0911

There is a neurological disease called **"kuru,"** which can be spread by **eating human flesh.** #0912

... However, **picking your nose** and eating snot is believed to actually **help your immune system.** #0913

201

8 facts about ROTTEN FOOD

Sardinian casu marzu cheese has maggots put in it on purpose … #0914

… People eat the cheese while the **MAGGOTS** are still alive … #0915

… It gets its special flavor from their poop. #0916

CIDER-MAKERS used to add some **MEAT TO THEIR APPLE** and water mixture. As the **MEAT ROTTED,** it helped the mixture turn to cider … #0917

… The meat was usually **livestock,** but sometimes it came from **rats** that had fallen into the barrels. #0918

Salami develops a mold around its casing while it's being made. The **mold is often left on** to give it flavor. #0919

In Thailand, you may be served **"stinky meat"**— game animal meat with the maggots left in it. #0920

Some winemakers use moldy grapes to make sweet wines such as **TOKAY OR SAUTERNES.** #0921

13 facts about SMELLY FOOD

The **smelliest fruit is the durian,** a spiky fruit from southeast Asia. It has been described as **"smelling of stale vomit and sewage,"** but it is supposed to be **VERY TASTY!** #0922

In Korea, STINKY TOFU is a **popular snack,** made of fermented soybeans, vegetables, and meat. #0923

Bombay duck isn't duck. It's a stinky, dried Indian fish famous for its funny name **(bummalo)** and its awful smell. #0924

KOPI LUWAK, the world's most expensive coffee, is made from coffee beans eaten and then pooped out by a small mammal called a **PALM CIVET.** #0925

It is eaten by making a **HOLE IN THE NECK** and sucking the juices out. #0927

KIVIAK is an Inuit meal made by stuffing 500 birds into **the body of a seal ...** #0926 ··········➤ ...

White truffles are **EDIBLE FUNGI** that sell for thousands of dollars per pound, despite their strange earthy, moldy smell. #0928

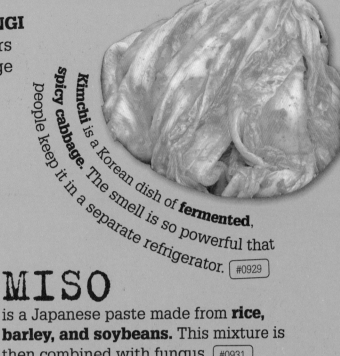

Kinchi is a Korean dish of **fermented, spicy cabbage.** The smell is so powerful that people keep it in a separate refrigerator. #0929

Stinking Bishop has been voted the **smelliest cheese in Britain.** It is soaked in fermented pears to give it its strong smell. #0930

MISO

is a Japanese paste made from **rice, barley, and soybeans.** This mixture is then combined with fungus. #0931

In China, people leave **EGGS TO ROT** for months, or even years, turning the yolks

DARK GREEN

and smelly, before eating them. #0932

Surströmming is a Swedish dish of fermented herring, and is thought to be the **world's smelliest food.** #0933

A **Limburger sandwich** is filled with **raw onion, mustard,** and **Limburger cheese,** which smells like BODY ODOR. #0934

11 FACTS ABOUT AWFUL OFFAL

Offal dishes are a popular delicacy in many countries. Offal is the **internal organs and guts of an animal.**

#0935

In Brazil, traditional feijoada **(PORK AND BEAN STEW)** sometimes includes the **EARS, FEET,** and **TAIL** of a pig. #0936

Animal tongue
can be eaten baked, pickled, or as slices of cold sandwich meat. #0937

The rubbery lining of a cow's stomach is called **tripe,** and can be eaten in different forms depending on which of the three stomach chambers it comes from ...

#0938

... **Blanket tripe** comes from the first, **honeycomb tripe** from the second, and **book tripe** from the third. #0939

Blood soup is popular in many places around the world. **CZERNINA** is a **Polish soup** made from **DUCK BLOOD** and **HAEJANGGUK** is a **Korean soup** made from **OX BLOOD.**

#0940

Black pudding is a blood sausage cooked until it has gone solid.

#0941

Chefs often use caul fat, a thin animal stomach lining, to wrap around meat when cooking. #0942

HEAD CHEESE, or brawn, is meat from the head of a pig set in jelly.

#0943

Some recipes for meatballs use a pig's liver, lungs, and heart.

#0944

ANIMAL BRAINS are also eaten around the world. In France, CERVELLE DE VEAU is a dish made from **calf's brains,** while **ox brain fritters are popular in Cuba.**

#0945

6 FACTS ABOUT STRANGE STOMACH CONTENTS

In the U.S., nearly **5,000 OBJECTS** have been **accidentally left inside patients** during surgery in the last 20 years. #0946

"Pica" is the urge to eat nonfoods such as CHALK, COAL, DIRT, OR SAND. #0947

The most common objects left **inside people** were **sponges,** but **scalpels** and **scissors** have also been left inside. #0948

208

A **man's arm,** a **crocodile head, copper wire,** and a **pet dog** have all been found inside **SHARKS.** #0949

A **pet dog,** a **ball,** and a **diaper** have been found in the stomach of an Australian crocodile. #0950

One gray whale was found with a stomach **full of trash,** including **plastic bags** and golf balls. #0951

8 BIZARRE THINGS TO EAT

In 2012, an Australian girl ate a toy that expands in water. It **blocked her intestine** and had to be removed by surgery. #0952

In 2011, 28-year-old Kuleshwar Singh was found to have swallowed **421 COINS**, which had to be removed by a surgeon. #0955

A hairball weighing **11 lb** was found in an 18-year-old American girl's stomach after she had been eating her own hair **FOR 5 YEARS.** #0953

A toddler was admitted to hospital with three pieces of his older sibling's **magnetic building set** inside him. He'd thought they were candy. #0954

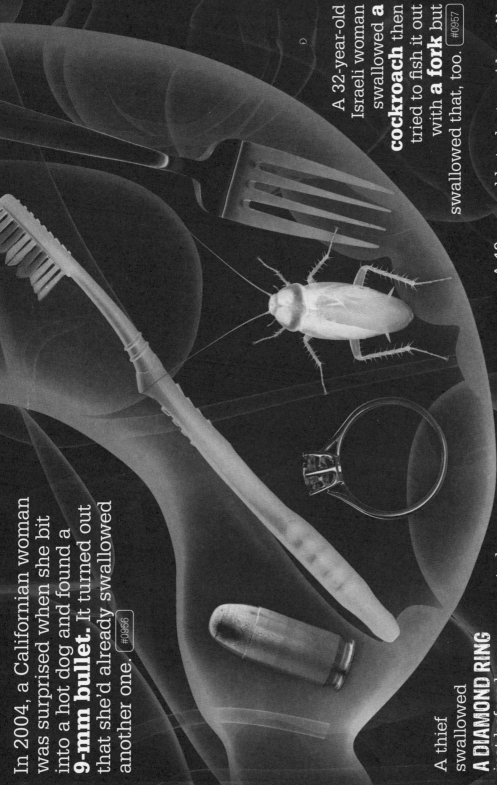

In 2004, a Californian woman was surprised when she bit into a hot dog and found a **9-mm bullet.** It turned out that she'd already swallowed another one. #0956

A thief swallowed **A DIAMOND RING** just before he was arrested. The jeweler eventually got the ring back after it had been through the thief's digestive system. #0958

A 32-year-old Israeli woman swallowed **a cockroach** then tried to fish it out with **a fork** but swallowed that, too. #0957

A 19-year-old student accidentally swallowed her **TOOTHBRUSH** while cleaning her tongue. #0959

9 facts about bugs found in food

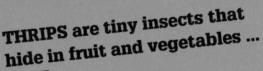

THRIPS are tiny insects that hide in fruit and vegetables ... #0960

... Sometimes they are not killed by pesticides so you will probably **swallow a few of them in your dinner.** #0961

Caterpillars live in spinach, AND LAY EGGS ON IT. You will probably find **some larvae on any fresh spinach.** #0962

There are about **30** **aphids (greenfly)** in every **4 oz** of **Brussels sprouts.** #0964

OREGANO can legally contain up to **1,250** INSECT FRAGMENTS PER **10 g.** #0963

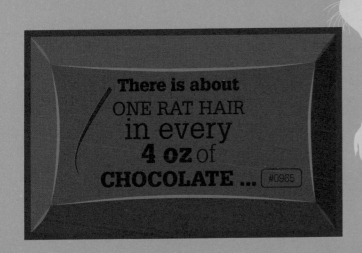

There is about **ONE RAT HAIR** in every **4 oz** of **CHOCOLATE** ... #0965

... but there may be up to **FIVE rodent hairs** in every **jar of peanut butter.** #0966

CINNAMON
can carry up to
1 milligram
of animal poop per pound.
#0967

There may be up to **19 tiny maggots** and **74 mites** in a regular **can of mushrooms.** #0968

213

12 STOMACH-CHURNING FACTS ABOUT FOOD INGREDIENTS

L-cysteine is added to processed bread to make the dough stronger. **It can come from bird feathers, pig hair, or even human hair.** #0969

CELLULOSE is used to make paper and cotton, but it can also be used as a **fat substitute** or source of fiber in some **processed foods.** #0970

Carmine is a red coloring used in CRANBERRY JUICE. It's made from an **acid found in some insects.** #0971

Castoreum, an ingredient used to add a **raspberry flavor,** is a **bitter, smelly brown liquid** that comes from a **gland in a beaver's bottom.** #0972

ISINGLASS stops beer going cloudy. It is made from dried fish bladders. #0973

Sheep make a substance called lanolin, an oil that can be found in many **COSMETICS** and some brands of **CHEWING GUM.** #0974

Up to **30 percent of the weight of a frozen chicken** comes from salt water injected into it. #0975

Vegetable oil with added bromine is a common ingredient in soda. Bromine is also used to keep plastics from catching fire. #0976

Many cheeses are produced using **rennet,** which comes from **the stomach of a young cow.** #0977

Shellac, derived from the **female lac bug,** makes a great wood primer. It can also be used to make **CANDIES** or fruit look shiny. #0978

Silicon dioxide is the main chemical in **SAND** but is also used to keep powdered food, such as table salt, from **GOING LUMPY.** #0980

Ammonia is used on **beef trimmings to kill bacteria and remove fat.** The treated meat **is then added to other beef products.** #0979

10 eye-watering SPICE facts

Moruga Scorpion 2,000,000 SHU

The Scoville scale measures the strength (hotness) of chili peppers, or how much they **burn your mouth.**

#0981

Bell Pepper 0 SHU (Scoville heat unit)

The hottest chili pepper ever recorded was a **TRINIDAD MORUGA SCORPION,** which reached over 2 million on the Scoville scale.

#0982

Chili peppers contain **capsaicin, a chemical that irritates human tissue.** If you touch a chili and then touch anywhere on your body that is sensitive, it will burn.

#0983

Bile is a bitter liquid produced by the liver, which helps the body to DIGEST FAT. Eating ginger can help increase bile production.

#0984

Garlic is used to flavor many foods, but it contains a substance called allyl methyl sulfide, which **makes your breath smell ....**

#0985

... This garlicky smell can even come out in **YOUR SWEAT.**

#0986

The ancient Greeks used mustard paste to **TREAT TOOTHACHE.**

#0987

In 2013, a New York restaurant served a curry so fiery that chefs **wore gas masks** to prepare it ... #0988

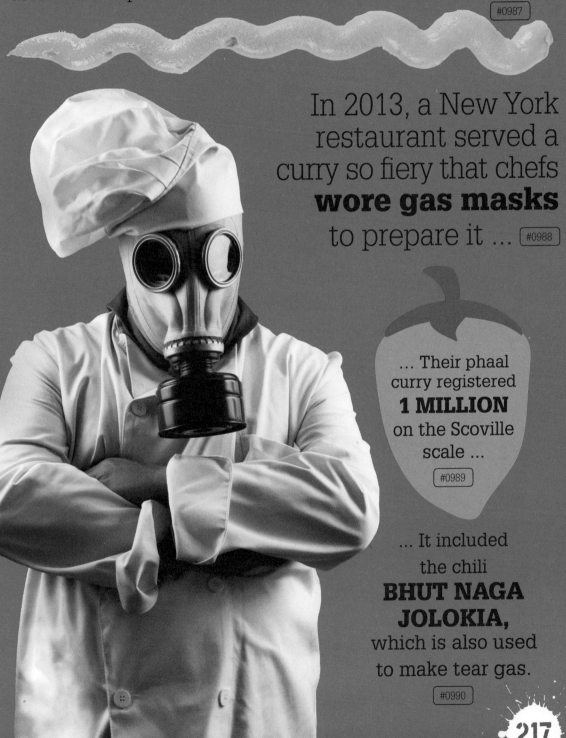

... Their phaal curry registered **1 MILLION** on the Scoville scale ...

#0989

... It included the chili **BHUT NAGA JOLOKIA,** which is also used to make tear gas.

#0990

10 FACTS ABOUT STRANGE VEGETABLES

If you eat too many carrots, it can cause **carotenemia** and parts of your skin will turn orange. However, it is not dangerous to your health. #0991

Cassava is a root crop that should not be eaten raw because it contains **cyanide**, which can cause paralysis if eaten. #0992

Nopal is a vegetable made from the **prickly pear cactus,** with the spiky spines removed. #0993

Beeturia is when your **pee comes out pink** from eating too much beetroot. #0994

Fiddleheads are a curly green vegetable eaten in New England. They look like **worms.** #0995

Salsify is a root vegetable that **tastes** quite like **oysters**. #0996

Dulse is a **red alga** that hangs from shorelines like seaweed. It is a popular snack in Ireland and Iceland. #0997

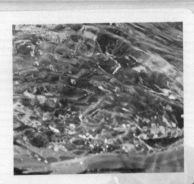

In southeast Asia **cha om** is put in omelets, giving off a **horrid whiff** before it is cooked. #0998

Peter Glazebrook, a grower of **giant vegetables**, grew an **18-lb onion**. #0999

Chinese artichokes look like **little insects,** but are usually pickled and put in salads. #1000

INDEX

ACKNOWLEDGMENTS

t = top, b = bottom, l = left, r = right, c = center

1tl Pdtnc/Dreamstime.com, 1b Eric Issellee/Shutterstock.com, 2 all arlindo71/istockphoto.com, 4tr Dreamstime.com, 4c istockphoto.com, 4b Asier Villafrance/Shutterstock.com, 5tr Milos Luzanin/Shutterstock.com, 5crt sailko/Creative Commons Attribution-Share Alike 3.0, 5crb Plume Photography/Shutterstock.com, 5br p.studio66/Shutterstock.com, 6-7 D. Kucharski K. Kurchaska/Shutterstock.com, 8l Dragon_fang/Dreamstime.com, 9r Nruboc/Dreamstime.com, 10tl sdominick/istockphoto.com, 12 artjazz/Shutterstock.com, 13t Dreamstime.com, 14bl chikapylka/Shutterstock.com, 15c Dreamstime.com, 16tr Shell114/Shutterstock.com, 16cl princessdloft/istockphoto.com, 17tl Eleonora Kolomiyets/Shutterstock.com, 17br gorilla images/Shutterstock.com, 18-19 Shutterstock.com, 19tr tehcheesiang/Shutterstock.com, 20l Dreamstime.com, 21bl Bevan Goldswain/Shutterstock.com, 22-23 Rocky Mountain Laboratories, NIAID, NIH, 24bl Fotosmurf02/Dreamstime.com, 25tr Tatappo/Dreamstime.com, 26-27tc Martan/Shutterstock.com, 27r Dreamstime.com, 29tr Dreamstime.com, 29br lucato/istockphoto.com, 30-31 picsfive/Shutterstock.com, 32l Fotograf77/Dreamstime.com, 33t istockphoto.com, 35r Monkey Business Images/Shutterstock.com, 36-37 Freddy Thuerig/Shutterstock.com, 38b Emi/Shutterstock.com, 39tr Kurt/Shutterstock.com, 39br Shane White/Shutterstock.com, 40br r.classen/Shutterstock.com, 41tr Carolina Smith/Dreamstime.com, 43bl Mairead/Dreamstime.com, 45tr Galyna Andrushka/Shutterstock.com, 47tr Dreamstime.com, 48tl Darrenp/Shutterstock.com, 49tc istockphoto.com, 50b Dreamstime.com, 51bl nicolas.voisin44/Shutterstock.com, 52bl James H. Robinson/Science Photo Library, 53tc Jubal Harshaw/Shutterstock.com, 54c Griffin024/Dreamstime.com, 54bl SPL, 55tr Aughty/Dreamstime.com, 55br FLPA/Lynwood Chace, 55bl stoykovic/Shutterstock.com, 56-57 istockphoto.com, 56tc Paul Fleet/Dreamstime.com, 56bc Peter Waters/Shutterstock.com, 57tc Xenobug/Dreamstime.com, 57c ex0rzist/Dreamstime.com, 58t Blanscape/Dreamstime.com, 58-59b Clearviewstock/Dreamstime.com, 60tr Pdtrc/Dreamstime.com, 60bl Dan Gerber/Shutterstock.com, 61c Lisa S./Shutterstock.com, 61b Prillfoto/Dreamstime.com, 63b arlindo71/istockphoto.com, 64tr Edd48/Creative Commons Attribution-Share Alike 3.0, 65bl Diane Bray/Creative Commons Attribution-Share Alike 3.0, 65tr NOAA, 66-67 Eris Isselee/Shutterstock.com, 67tr Maksym Boderchuk/Shutterstock.com, 68-69 Everett Collection/Shutterstock.com, 70b Christophe Boisvieux/Corbis, 72-73b Asier Villafranca/Shutterstock.com, 75r Leswrona/Dreamstime.com, 76-77 pzAxe/Shutterstock.com, 76c Cosmin Manci/Shutterstock.com, 82b Maksym Bonderchuk/Shutterstock.com, 83bl Elenathewise/Dreamstime.com, 84bl Lukiyanova Natalia/Shutterstock.com, 84-85b elnavegante/Shutterstock.com, 87b exopixel/Shutterstock.com, 89t Antonio Abignani/Shutterstock.com, 89cr Nicemonkey/Shutterstock.com, 89b Elfim Belousov/Shutterstock.com, 93cl Velazquez77/Shutterstock.com, 94b Bob Thomas/Popperfoto/Getty, 96-97 Igor Lateci/Shutterstock.com, 96bc Baemcr/Dreamstime.com, 98-99 Anatolich/Shutterstock.com, 101b Cathy Keifer/Shutterstock.com, 103t koya979/Shutterstock.com, 103cl Chaoss/Dreamstime.com, 105cr photastic/Shutterstock.com, 106b Ungarf/Dreamstime.com, 107 Milos Luzanin/Shutterstock.com, 109tr cynoclub/Shutterstock.com, 109bl huronphoto/istockphoto.com, 110cr vdeenko/Shutterstock.com, 111tr Didier Descouens/Creative Commons Attribution-Share Alike 3.0, 111cb Dimasobko/Dreamstime.com, 112bl Kkaplin/Dreamstime.com, 113tr Icholakov/Dreasmtime.com, 113br Marafona738/Dreasmtime.com, 115tc okili77/Shutterstock.com, 115bl Stuart Jenner/Shutterstock.com, 116-117 Sergey Nivens/Shutterstock.com, 116cr monticello/Shutterstock.com, 117tc Emley Smith/Shutterstock.com, 117br vnovikov/Shutterstock.com, 118-119 Makson Kabakov/Shutterstock.com, 118br Evgeny Karandanyev/Shutterstock.com, 119bl Alexander Ryanbintov/Shutterstock.com, 120b ollyy/Shutterstock.com, 121tr (iPad) FrankGaertner/Shutterstock.com, 121tr (Google Glass) Tedeytan/Creative Commons Attribution-Share Alike 2.0, 121b Andrey_Popov/Shutterstock.com, 122-123 Phiseksit/Shutterstock.com, 124-125c NASA, 125t Robynrg/Shutterstock.com, 125br Dvmsimages/Dreamstime.com, 126tl Sirophat/Shutterstock.com, 126bl, br, 127 all NASA, 128-129 zhuda/Shutterstock.com, 130-131ODM/Shutterstock.com, 130-131 (leaves) smuay/Shutterstock.com, 131r Arun Roisri/Shutterstock.com, 132br Seleznev Oleg/Shutterstock.com, 132-133c cglade/istockphoto.com, 133bl Nightowiza/Dreamstime.com, 133r Annavee/Shutterstock.com, 134b Olga Dalynenko/Shutterstock.com, 135tr saluha/istockphoto.com, 135cr Artiesky/Shutterstock.com, 135bl Vovashevchuk/Dreamstime.com, 136-137 all Dreamstime.com, 138-139b Dreamstime.com, 139tr Anita Ponne/Shutterstock.com, 140tr nevenm/Shutterstock.com, 140-141b Dennis M. Sabangan/epa/Corbis, 142-143 Robert Adrian Hillman/Shutterstock.com, 144-145 Dreamstime.com, 144-145b Shutterstock.com, 146 rangizzz/Shutterstock.com, 146cl Chaoss/Dreamstime.com, 148-149 all Shutterstock.com, 152b Aero17/Dreamstime.com, 152cl Studiovin/Shutterstock.com, 154bl Michael Rosskothen/Shutterstock.com, 155tr Africa Studio/Shutterstock.com, 155cr Victor Prymachenko/Shutterstock.com, 156b Sailko/Creative Commons Attribution-Share Alike 3.0, 157b Infomages/Shutterstock.com, 158-159 Lena Lir/Shutterstock.com, 160l AFP Getty, 161t Gauravmasand/Dreamstime.com, 162-163 Dreamstime.com, 164 hxdbzxy/Shutterstock.com, 165 Dragana Gerasimoski/Shutterstock.com, 166c Edward Westmacott/Shutterstock.com, 167tr Anniwalz/Dreamstime.com, 167b Getty Images, 168br Fechetm/Dreamstime.com, 171tr Norman Poggon/Shutterstock.com, 171br jadimages/Shutterstock.com, 174tl Hellen Sergeyeva/Shutterstock.com, 175br Ryzhkov Alexandr/Shutterstock.com, 177t xpixel/Shutterstock.com, 177bl Plume Phtography/Shutterstock.com, 178bl mrubic/Shutterstock.com, 178-179 Shutterstock.com, 179tr Planctonvideo/Dreamstime.com, 180l wrangler/Shutterstock.com, 181tr Shutterstock.com, 181b travellight/Shutterstock.com, 182br chlppix/Shutterstock.com, 183tl Everett Collection/Shutterstock.com, 184tl Sarah Marchant/Shutterstock.com, 185b Angonius/Shutterstock.com, 186bl Steve Bower/Shutterstock.com, 188-189 FiledIMAGE/Shutterstock.com, 190bl meunierd/Shutterstock.com, 190-191c Donald Hoen/Creative Commons Attribution 2.0, 191tr Kostov/Shutterstock.com, 191br p.studio66/Shutterstock.com, 192bl kati1313/Dreamstime.com, 193tr Disorderly/Dreamstime.com, 194tl Jinga/Shutterstock.com, 194-195 Shutterstock.com, 197cl Triff/Shutterstock.com, 197tr igor.stevanovic/Shutterstock.com, 198bl pick/Shutterstock.com, 199cl bitt24/Shutterstock.com, 199cr erlire74/Shutterstock.com, 200-201 all Shutterstock.com, 202tl Shardan/Creative Commons Attribution-Share Alike 2.5, 203tr gcpics/Shutterstock.com, 203c dabjola/Shutterstock.com, 203b LockStockBob/Shutterstock.com, 204c Eldred Lm/Shutterstock.com, 204b Nordling/Shutterstock.com, 205tr Jiang Hongyan/Shutterstock.com, 205cl margouillat photo/Shutterstock.com, 205bl ArTono/Shutterstock.com, 206tl AnjelikaGR/Shutterstock.com, 207tr de2marco/Shutterstock.com, 207cl Mirabelle Pictures/Shutterstock.com, 208l f9photos/Shutterstock.com, 208cr Noraluca013/Shutterstock.com, 209 pattyphotoart/Shutterstock.com, 210-211 all Shutterstock.com, 212tl Sirikorn Techatabihop/Shutterstock.com, 213br antpkr/Shutterstock.com, 214tr Guzel Strudio/Shutterstock.com, 214bl fotofactory/Shutterstock.com, 214br Tim UR/Shutterstock.com, 215tr Stock Lite/Shutterstock.com, 215c Phil MacDonald/Shutterstock.com, 216tr Swapan Photography/Shutterstock.com, 216bl Andre S/Shutterstock.com, 217t Studio VIN/Shutterstock.com, 217l carlosdelacalle/Shutterstock.com, 218-219 Shutterstock.com, 218cl My Life Graphic/Shutterstock.com, 219tc Robert Taylor/Shutterstock.com, 219cr Piamsak Hansuri/Shutterstock.com